From Tactical to Strategic

Bringing HR to the forefront of business

Donald M. Herrmann, MBA, SHRM-SCP

Printed in the United States of America

ISBN: 979-8-9941112-0-8

Contents

A Message to the Reader: Unlocking HR's Full Potential

I started writing this book years ago because I strongly believe in the tremendous, often unused value that Human Resources can bring to a company. My first goal was straightforward: many HR professionals lacked a clear way to explain value using terms that senior executives actually care about.

As I gained more experience, I realized that transitioning to a high-value, strategic HR function is challenging due to persistent issues within organizations, problems that show up at all levels, including sometimes within the HR department itself.

The key obstacles that slow down the shift to Strategic HR include:

- **The Cost Center Mindset:** The outdated belief that employees are mainly a cost to be controlled, rather than the company's biggest source of competitive edge and growth. This view limits spending on people and focuses the department on daily paperwork.

- **Skepticism of Impact:** A reluctance to fully accept the clear link between talent strategy and financial success. Even when we present solid data proving that HR improvements, such as better training or stable leadership, directly increase performance, output, and profit, some leaders still doubt the strategic importance of HR.

- **Resistance to Data:** The tendency to ignore or push back against accurate information and serious analysis from the HR department. This is especially true when that data challenges existing methods or doesn't match what people already think HR should be doing.

It's important to note that these behaviors aren't limited to just senior executives. They are part of a wider resistance to change, and sometimes they appear inside the HR function itself, stopping us from fully becoming a strategic partner. This book is designed to provide you with the common language and financial proof necessary to overcome these roadblocks and ultimately establish HR as a critical driver of business value.

The Professional Village: Mentors, Colleagues, and Peers

This book is built upon the lessons, challenges, and insights gained over years of collaboration.

I owe a profound debt of gratitude to my mentors, who guided me through my career. Too numerous to name, and some didn't even know they were mentoring me. Your guidance on everything from HR to business, experiences, challenges, processes, and more has shaped the fundamental points within these pages.

To my colleagues and partners at the companies I have worked for or with, and the students I have taught, thank you for challenging my thinking and for being willing to test these frameworks in the real world.

The Editorial and Production Team

I am deeply grateful for the precision, expertise, and dedication of those who helped me along the way.

Glenda, Jerri, Lyndsey, Heather, Darryl, Wayne, Gordon, Emilio, Dawn, Katie, Diana, Jennifer, Mike, Pat, and many more all played a role, whether you know it or not.

Inspiration and the Road Ahead

Finally, to the HR Community and other business leaders who will pick up this book: This work is dedicated to your success. My hope is that it empowers you to elevate your function and bring the strategic value that people leaders are uniquely positioned to deliver.

AI created the images in this book, helped clarify sections of the writing, and Grammarly supported accuracy in grammar, punctuation, and spelling.

0.1 The Moment of Reckoning: Why HR Must Evolve or Perish

The core mission of this guide is to move HR out of the administrative 'tactical trap' and into a position of strategic influence. When HR makes this fundamental shift, it stops being a necessary expense and becomes a direct driver of profit, growth, and risk reduction. Strategic HR connects every people decision to core business outcomes and measures success in dollars, not just activities. For too long, HR teams have been stuck in the tactical trap: handling forms, compliance, and payroll; running programs without linking them to financial outcomes; and reporting on activity rather than business impact. This is what makes HR appear as a cost center. The strategic opportunity is clear: HR becomes a value driver when it learns to speak the language of cost, revenue, and risk, helping executive leaders make faster, smarter workforce decisions for maximum return. This manual provides the exact plan, steps, and communication tools needed to make this transition a financial must-do for the entire organization.

Today's business world is shaped by three key factors: technology is changing at an unprecedented rate, global competition is intense, and owners and investors continually demand improved performance for less money. As a result, every company department is being closely monitored. The finance team must predict the future, operations must be streamlined, and the technology team must be flexible.

But HR has a major problem. While company leaders all agree that "people are our greatest asset," the HR department itself is often seen as a slow, necessary annoyance cost center focused on following rules, running payroll, and handling paperwork. This view is fair because HR activities typically fail to directly connect to the Profit and Loss (P&L) statement.

The time for this kind of reactive, administrative work is over. The biggest challenges companies face now, such as skills becoming obsolete due to Artificial Intelligence, the need for highly flexible company structures, and competing globally for top talent, are all fundamentally people-related problems. If HR remains stuck in outdated policies and paperwork, it won't just fail to help; it will hinder the company's success. Tactical (old-school) HR will struggle to cope with the weight of these new challenges. Strategic HR is the only function ready to ensure the organization not only survives but also wins.

The Outside Pressure that Demands a Strategic Shift

To understand why this change is so important, you must first consider the pressure the economy is putting on your company. This isn't about office politics; it's about staying in business.

1. Skills Change Faster: Technology now changes in months, not years. A specialized skill that gave you an advantage a few years ago might be automated or widely available next quarter. The real challenge is no longer *hiring* people; it's retaining them. It's forecasting when your current staff's skills will become outdated and planning for new training or hiring years in advance. Tactical HR waits until a job opens up. Strategic HR studies the obsolescence curve (how quickly skills become obsolete) for most employees and fills that skills gap years in advance. Ignoring this is a significant, measurable risk of not having the right people.

2. Owner Pressure to Cut Costs: Every dollar spent on overhead, including HR staff and systems, is measured against profit goals. If HR cannot demonstrate a clear return on investment (ROI), its work is often viewed as an expense that should be cut. The only way to stop budget cuts is to change HR spending from a simple expense line into a measurable capital investment that brings in more revenue or saves more money than it costs. This requires HR to talk in financial terms.

3. The Complexity of Global and Remote Work: Managing teams that are spread out, diverse, and often contracted brings major headaches for rule-following and cultural blending that old-school administrative HR can't handle. Tactical HR sees remote work as just a policy headache. Strategic HR sees it as a way to get a competitive edge in talent, setting up cultural rules and performance goals that ensure quality and productivity across different regions.

Case Study: The Retail Giant's Digital Failure: A large retail company, facing a serious threat from online shopping, decided to start a $500 million project to go digital. The tactical HR department was simply told to hire 1,000 new digital experts. They efficiently ran the hiring process and tracked applications. However, they failed to conduct a talent forecast for their 10,000 existing corporate employees. Strategic HR would have known that 30% of the current roles (such as purchasing and middle management) required more digital skills to support the new platform, and 15% were likely to be eliminated soon. By focusing solely on new hiring (a tactical move) and neglecting internal training and restructuring (a strategic move), the company ultimately ended up with a new digital platform that the existing staff couldn't effectively use. This resulted in a two-year project delay and a loss of $1 billion in company value. The failure was a people problem managed by a tactical HR team.

0.2 The Purpose of This Guide: Your Complete Transformation Blueprint

This guide is not a long essay about general ideas. It is a working manual, step-by-step roadmap for the HR professional who is ready to make a huge change. It accepts that the move from Tactical to Strategic is a large project with three separate, but connected, battles: the fight for internal capacity (time), the fight for external credibility (with the CEO), and the fight for peer collaboration (with other department heads).

The Three Guarantees of This Manual

1. The Framework (The "How"): Part I lays out the three-phase plan for change. It starts with the necessary job of "cleaning house" to create the time you need for strategy. You can't think strategically if you are drowning in paperwork. Then, it moves on to mastering predictive data, transitioning from merely reporting on the past (what happened last quarter) to forecasting the future (what will happen in three years).

2. The Language (The "What to Say"): The biggest barrier to HR influence is how HR talks. This guide trains you to stop talking about "mood," "engagement," and "employee happiness" and start talking about financial impact: Cost, Revenue, and Risk. Every single idea you propose, from a new training program to a new pay system, must be looked at through the P&L statement. The goal is to change the conversation from "Do we have to do this?" to "What is the ROI (Return on Investment) on this spending?"

3. The Strategy (The "How to Win"): This transformation is highly political. Part II deals with the skepticism you will face from company leaders, offering the Proof-of-Concept (PoC) Strategy as the proven way to build trust and get budget approval. Part III tackles the 'turf war' problems that pop up when HR gains power, giving you ways to build shared ownership and turn skeptical department heads into willing partners.

Actionable Insight: The Promise of the New Language. After finishing this guide, you will be ready to replace your old, ineffective HR phrases with financially sound ones:

Ineffective Tactical Statement	Financially Strategic Equivalent
"We need to update our benefits package to improve morale."	"Our current benefits package, combined with our 35% regrettable turnover, is causing an annual $1.2 million talent leakage risk; a targeted investment of $150,000 in a new package is expected to cut that loss by 10%, giving us a 7:1 ROI."
"Managers need leadership training."	"Bad management is causing a 14-week Time-to-Productivity (TTTP) average for new hires. This delay risks a $2.5 million revenue miss by pushing back our Q4 product launch. Training is needed to speed up TTTP to 10 weeks."
"We need a better performance review process."	"Our current, unclear review process doesn't give us the data we need to identify and invest in our Critical Roles. This puts 7 of our 10 executive positions at high Succession Readiness Risk, which threatens the stability of the entire company."

0.3 The Anatomy of the Strategic Shift: Capacity, Capability, Credibility

The shift is a step-by-step process. Trying to skip the early stages, such as going straight for the CEO's attention without first having the necessary capacity, is the number one reason these efforts fail. The plan in this guide is built on three main pillars that must be built in order.

Pillar 1: Capacity (The Freedom to Think)

The Challenge: The tactical HR team is always busy but never seems to get the most important work done. They spend 60–80% of their time on transactional, administrative tasks that create zero strategic value. This lost time stops them from doing high-level analysis.

The Solution: Phase 1, "Assess and Clean House," focuses on completely changing this ratio. This is the Process-Time-Cost Analysis, figuring out the exact dollar cost of every hour spent on manual administrative tasks (like paper filing or manually checking timecards). The goal is to quickly automate, outsource, or eliminate these tasks to reduce administrative time to under 10%. This creates time capacity, allowing the HR team to stop pushing paper and start analyzing data. Importantly, the money saved by this automation is the first real ROI that HR can show the CFO.

Deeper Explanation for the Non-Professional: Capacity is simply time. Think of a talented carpenter who is excellent at complex jobs but spends 95% of his day answering phone calls and sorting invoices. The company pays him a high salary, but it only gets 5% of his valuable skills. Your HR team is the same. Until you automate the "phone calls and invoices" part of HR, you will never use their true potential. The first, required step is to stop wasting time on manual work.

Pillar 2: Capability (The Ability to Predict)

The Challenge: Once the team has free time (Capacity), they must have the skills to use it well. Tactical HR measures activity (like, "We trained people for 1,000 hours"). Strategic HR measures impact (like, "That training cut production errors by 15%"). This shift requires mastering data and turning simple numbers into predictions.

The Solution: Phase 2, "Mastering the Data," sets up the key strategic metrics: Time-to-Productivity (TTTP), Cost of Regrettable Turnover, and Revenue Per Employee. This phase teaches the HR leader and their team how to build a Talent Forecast, a forward-looking 3–5-year analysis that answers the question: "Do we have the people and skills we need to execute the CEO's future plan?" The focus is on data storytelling, turning complex data into a concise business story linked directly to a financial outcome (e.g., "The slow TTTP is the main reason the Alpha Project is delayed"). Capability is the ability to utilize data to stop reporting the past and start predicting risk.

Pillar 3: Credibility (The License to Operate)

The Challenge: Having the time (Capacity) and the data skills (Capability) isn't enough if the executive team doesn't trust your judgment or value your opinion. Credibility is earned by consistently delivering measurable financial results.

The Solution: Phase 3, "Building the Strategic Portfolio," is where the HR leader officially becomes a Trusted Advisor. This involves two key actions: holding formal **Alignment Workshops** with the executive team to ensure the HR strategy aligns perfectly with the business strategy and utilizing Proof-of-Concept (PoC) projects strategically. The PoC is a high-profile, small, and contained intervention designed to solve the CEO's most immediate problem (like high turnover in the critical Sales team). By addressing a noticeable problem, demonstrating the exact dollar savings, and presenting a measurable "before-and-after" financial result, the HR leader earns the right to propose significant, long-term strategic investments.

Case Study: The Mid-Sized Tech Firm's Turnaround. A 600-employee e-commerce logistics company had an HR team that was always rushing to fix emergencies. Their transformation followed the three pillars exactly:

- **Capacity:** They first bought a simple, ready-to-use HRIS system, moving all benefits and time-off requests to employee self-service. This freed up two full-time HR administrators, resulting in $140,000 in annual savings. (Pillar 1 achieved).

- **Capability:** The freed-up staff were trained to analyze exit interview data and found their regrettable turnover cost was $1.1 million per year. They then created a 3-year Talent Forecast showing they would not have enough Data Engineers for their next growth phase. (Pillar 2 achieved).

- **Credibility:** The CEO was complaining about turnover in the newly bought Western Operations division. HR suggested a 90-day PoC: a focused manager training program for only that division, costing $15,000. After 90 days, the annual turnover rate dropped from 42% to 25%. HR showed the CFO a report projecting an annual savings of $450,000 in replacement costs. This PoC success was used to get approval for a $500,000 company-wide manager development program. (Pillar 3 achieved).

0.4 Deconstructing the "Soft Stuff" Critique: Quantifying Human Capital Risk

The biggest mental wall for HR professionals is the common executive dismissal that HR only deals with "soft stuff" vague ideas like culture, morale, and engagement that supposedly don't belong in a serious financial discussion.

The strategic HR leader must destroy this false idea by proving that every single "soft" HR variable has a direct, measurable, and "hard" financial link.

- **Culture is not "touchy-feely," it is the Operating System of Results.** A toxic culture immediately leads to measurable outcomes: more employee arguments (wasting manager time), higher injury rates (increasing insurance costs), and lower quality scores (leading to wasted work and lost customers). Strategic HR manages culture with the same strictness that Operations manages its physical machines.

- **Engagement is not "happiness," it is Project Velocity.** Disengaged employees work more slowly, make more mistakes, and are less likely to go the extra mile. Studies show that high-trust teams consistently finish projects faster because they waste less time on internal arguing and checking each other's work. The strategic HR leader compares the internal engagement score with the average project time in the Research & Development department. The difference in completion time is a direct translation of engagement into faster revenue.

- **Inclusion is not just following rules, it is Innovation Insurance.** Diverse teams, when supported by an inclusive culture, are proven to generate more successful ideas, develop better product features, and achieve superior problem-solving. By failing to build an inclusive culture, the company is actively holding back its innovation, creating a measurable risk of being left behind by competitors.

Example Translation: Abstract HR Concepts to Financial Impact

The following table shows the required translation for every HR idea:

Abstract HR Concept (Avoid)	Hard Business Consequence (Focus)	Financial/Risk Translation
Morale/Employee Satisfaction	Regrettable Turnover (Losing Company Knowledge)	Cost of Replacement (1.5 times salary)

Team Conflict/Poor Communication	Project Delay and Rework	Lost Revenue/Increased Cost of Production
Leadership Development Need	Time-to-Productivity (TTTP) Lag	Delayed Revenue Contribution
Lack of Succession Planning	Talent Risk	(Relying on one person too much)

0.5 Navigating the Internal Landscape: The CEO and the Peer Challenge

The transformation of HR requires securing two separate, crucial alliances within the executive suite. Part II and Part III of this guide are dedicated to navigating the political and communication complexity of these challenges.

The CEO Filter: The Financial ROI

The CEO, President, or Investor-Owner operates with a simple, rigorous filter: Show me the money. They are driven by market pressures, quarterly results, and the long-term protection of enterprise value. They are often the most difficult person to convince because they are the most insulated from the day-to-day administrative burdens that consume the tactical HR team.

To succeed with the CEO, the HR leader must demonstrate:

- **Predictive Insight:** The ability to forecast future talent risks before they materialize on the P&L.

- **Concise Currency:** Proposals must be distilled into a single page or three slides that focus relentlessly on the ROI; the return on the human capital investment.

- **External Context:** The ability to frame HR initiatives as necessary "due diligence" against competitive threats or market-driven talent wars.

This is the art of the Investor Mindset: treating talent not as a resource to be managed, but as a capital asset to be invested in, developed, and protected against loss.

The Peer Challenge: Turf Wars and Zero-Sum Fallacy

When HR successfully transforms and begins to wield strategic influence, friction often emerges with peer functional leaders (e.g., the CFO, the VP of Operations, the CTO). This friction stems from a zero-sum fallacy: the perception that HR's gain in influence means a loss of autonomy or budget control for their department.

For example:

- The CFO may resist HR's new metrics (e.g., "Turnover Cost") because they compete with traditional financial measures.

- The VP of Operations may resist standardized recruiting or training processes because they perceive them as "unnecessary bureaucracy" that slows down their operational velocity.

This resistance must be overcome by demonstrating that strategic HR is about enlarging the pie for everyone. The VP of Operations doesn't lose autonomy; they gain a highly-trained, stable workforce that reduces their scrap rate and increases production quality. The CFO doesn't lose control; they gain an early warning system against massive, preventable talent risks. Part III provides the tactics to create Shared Metrics (e.g., Cost of Quality, owned jointly by Operations and HR) that eliminate turf wars by making collaboration the mandatory path to success for both functions.

0.6 Conclusion: The Ultimate Competitive Advantage

The journey outlined in this manual is challenging. It requires a fundamental shift in mindset, skillset, and organizational positioning. It requires the HR leader to transition from the comfort of process management to the rigorous, data-driven domain of financial and operational consulting.

The reward, however, is the establishment of the ultimate competitive advantage. In an era where product differentiation is short-lived and technology is rapidly copied, the only truly sustainable competitive advantage is a highly skilled, strategically aligned, and uniquely motivated workforce. The power to engineer that workforce, to protect that human capital asset, and to speak its value in the irrefutable language of finance rests entirely with the Strategic HR function.

Your mission, as detailed in the following chapters, is to stop being a necessary expense and become the essential core of the business itself. The power to define the future of your organization is now in your hands.

Chapter 1: The Tactical Trap and the Strategic Opportunity

Summary

This chapter establishes the core transition required of modern Human Resources: moving from transactional, administrative support to a Strategic HR function. Understanding and actively avoiding the Tactical Trap is a financial imperative for businesses seeking sustainable growth and a competitive advantage.

Step-by-Step Framework

The perception of Human Resources within a Small to Mid-sized Business (SMB) is often the single greatest determinant of that organization's ability to scale and maintain profit margins. For decades, HR's function has been largely defined by compliance and transactions: the annual flurry of paperwork, the monthly payroll cycle, and the reactive management of employee issues. This comfortable, yet debilitating routine, the execution of existing systems without the critical analysis of their financial or operational impact, is the Tactical Trap. This trap is highly dangerous because it presents a facade of productivity while leaving the business vulnerable to enormous, recurring costs associated with high turnover, compliance failures, and talent deficits.

The shift to Strategic HR is therefore not a discretionary upgrade; it is a financial imperative necessary for long-term competitive health. It transforms HR from a necessary cost handler into a critical mechanism for business growth. Strategic HR leverages data and forecasting to directly influence the outcomes on the company's Profit & Loss (P&L) statement, it unlocks new revenue streams by optimizing talent placement, decreases operational costs by proactively solving systemic problems, and mitigates catastrophic legal and talent risks. Recognizing that not all HR work carries the same value is paramount; the goal is to aggressively minimize time spent on basic maintenance to free up professional capacity for the proactive, predictive work that defines a value-driving asset.

1.1 The Three Faces of HR: A Framework for Strategic Transition

HR Allocation Shift

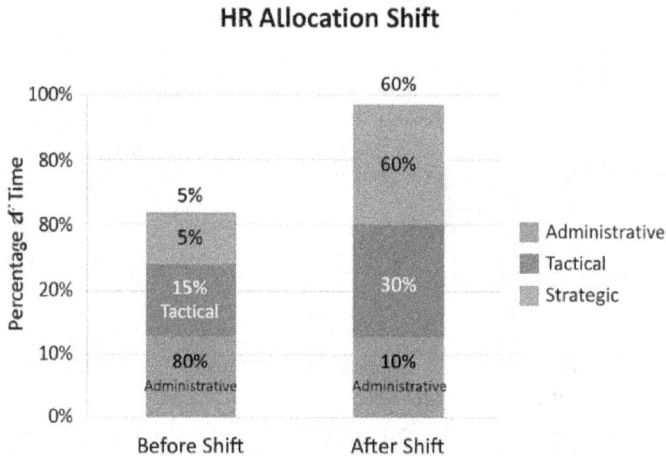

All HR activities can be categorized into three distinct faces: Administrative, Tactical, and Strategic. The journey to strategic partnership requires a deliberate effort to shift capacity from the first two faces to the third.

1. Administrative HR (The Cost Center)

What It Is: This is the reactive, transactional work, the absolute basic maintenance that keeps the lights on and the company legally compliant. It includes tasks that are often manual and repetitive, such as processing payroll, filing I-9 compliance paperwork, and performing routine data entry for new hires.

- **Analogy:** This is the plumbing of the organization. It is vital that the pipes don't burst, as failure leads to immediate fines or legal trouble, but the plumbing itself does not generate revenue or innovation.

- **Why It Must Be Minimized:** While essential for compliance, the dominance of this work is financially debilitating. When HR professionals spend the majority of their time on manual reconciliation, filing, and data entry, they are unable to address underlying systemic problems. The consequence is a function viewed by company leaders as simply an unavoidable cost center. Furthermore, this constant state of firefighting erodes HR's credibility, ensuring the team remains reactive and unable to engage with high-cost, recurring business problems, such as high injury rates or the strategic loss of key talent. The time lost to transactional burden is an opportunity cost.

- **The Strategic Objective:** The goal is to utilize automation and Employee Self-Service (ESS) to drive the time spent on Administrative HR down to less than 10% of the team's capacity. This technological shift is required to liberate professional capacity for value-driving work.

2. Tactical HR (The Program Runner)

What It Is: This involves executing routine, cyclical programs that are established and repeated annually, such as running the annual performance review cycle, managing open benefits enrollment, or mandatory annual training sessions.

- **Analogy:** This is like a train schedule. The HR team ensures the program runs on time and hits every milestone; success is measured by completion (e.g., "98% of reviews completed!"), not by impact on the business.

- **Why It Must Be Transformed:** Tactical work often provides a false sense of security and productivity. However, the fatal flaw is the failure to analyze the rich data generated by these programs to gain strategic insight. The team becomes highly efficient at managing the process, yet blind to the outcome. For example, if the performance review cycle is well-run but not connected to retention data, it is strategically worthless because it does not prevent the best people from leaving. Tactical HR limits organizational growth because it fails to connect its activities (e.g., training completion) to actual business outcomes (e.g., reduced accident rates, improved sales effectiveness), keeping the function trapped in a cycle of program management instead of value creation.

- **The Strategic Objective:** The goal is to transform every tactical program into a strategic initiative by asking the crucial question: "If this program's data (e.g., performance ratings) were linked to a key business outcome (e.g., employee turnover or customer service metrics), what actionable insight could be found that helps the company increase profit or reduce loss?"

3. Strategic HR (The Value Driver)

What It Is: This is the destination: work that is proactive and predictive. This function uses business data and business acumen (understanding of the company's financial goals and operational roadmap) to forecast future talent needs and align the workforce directly with the organization's long-term goals.

- **Analogy:** This is like the company's navigator. The Strategic HR function is looking years ahead, predicting where the company needs to go and ensuring the right vehicle (the talent pool) is ready for the journey.

- **The Financial Imperative:** This is the goal because Strategic HR links every people decision to the business's P&L statement. Instead of waiting for a crisis (such as high turnover or a sudden skill shortage), strategic HR anticipates it and launches preventive measures. The transformation is a financial necessity because it is the only way to proactively secure the talent needed for the organization's future revenue goals.

- **The Strategic Outcome:** HR becomes an active partner in achieving the company's biggest goals, focusing on increasing revenue, decreasing cost, and mitigating risk by effectively managing the human capital asset (the workforce).

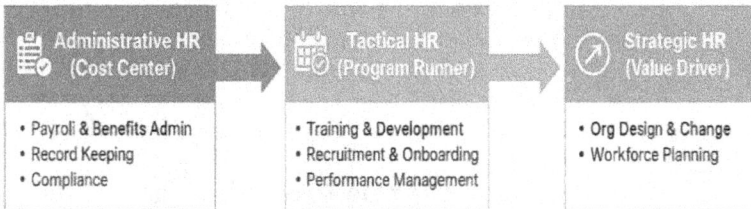

Administrative HR (Cost Center)	Tactical HR (Program Runner)	Strategic HR (Value Driver)
• Payroll & Benefits Admin • Record Keeping • Compliance	• Training & Development • Recruitment & Onboarding • Performance Management	• Org Design & Change • Workforce Planning

Sequential, Numbered Steps: The 5-Step Strategic Transition Framework

This framework provides a clear, actionable path to begin the essential shift from the Tactical Trap to the Strategic Opportunity.

1. **Quantify the Administrative Cost to Gain Capacity**

   o **Detailed Explanation:** Before any strategic planning can begin, the HR function must create its own internal capacity by eliminating administrative burden. This requires quantifying the manual effort into a hard dollar cost, which is the only evidence required to justify investment in automation. This process is called a Process-Time-Cost Analysis, and it translates inefficient processes into budgetary language. This analysis serves as proof that the *cost of inaction* (the cost of paying staff to do manual, repetitive data entry) is higher than the *cost of automation* (the cost of new software).

   o **Step-by-Step Action:**

     ▪ **A. List the Top 3 Time Sinks:** Time sinks are activities, processes, or behaviors that consume a disproportionate amount of time while delivering little or no meaningful value in return. They are not always obvious, and many persist simply because "that's how it's always been done." Identify the three transactional tasks consuming the most staff time (e.g., manual timecard approval, verifying benefits enrollment paperwork, organizing paper personnel files). These are the tasks that will yield the highest return on automation.

- **B. Estimate Time Spent:** For each HR role, estimate the average percentage of their workweek dedicated to these specific administrative tasks. Be rigorous, often tracking the actual time for a two-week period.

- **C. Calculate the Dollar Cost:** Determine the fully loaded salary (base salary plus the cost of benefits, usually an additional 20% to 30%) for the employee. Multiply this total cost by the estimated percentage of time spent.

  - **Example:** *A $50,000 salary HR Coordinator with a 25% benefits load costs the company $62,500 annually. If they spend 40% of their time on manual timecard reconciliation, the organizational cost for that one task is $25,000 ($62,500 X 0.40).* This quantified $25,000 cost immediately justifies a $15,000 Employee Self-Service (ESS) platform, demonstrating an immediate net savings.

2. **Anchor the Function to the CEO's #1 Goal.**

   - **Detailed Explanation:** Strategic HR does not operate in a vacuum. Its programs must be explicitly aligned with the business's most critical, top-line objective, the goal on which the CEO and executive team are measured. This ensures immediate relevance and maximum impact.

   - **Step-by-Step Action:**

- **A. Find the Anchor:** Consult with the CEO, CTO, or Sales Leader to identify the single biggest organizational priority: Is it "launch a new product line," "reduce operational expenses by 10%, " or "expand into a new market"?

- **B. Define the People Metric:** Immediately translate that organizational goal into a specific, measurable people problem. If the company goal is "Increase market share by 20%," the HR strategic focus must shift to "forecasting and acquiring the specialized talent needed to support that 20% market share growth." The function is now speaking the language of Revenue.

3. **Audit Tactical Programs for Strategic Data Gaps.**

   o **Detailed Explanation:** The most efficient way to become strategic is to leverage the data already being collected. This requires redesigning Tactical programs not for completion, but for analytical insight that solves a financial problem.

   o **Step-by-Step Action:**

     - **A. Identify a High-Cost Program:** Select an established cyclical program, such as the Annual Performance Review.

     - **B. Define the Strategic Gap:** Determine what critical business data is **not being linked** to the HR data. The largest and most significant gap is the lack of linkage between performance ratings (HR data) and compensation, as well as regrettable turnover (financial data).

- **C. Implement the Link:** Standardize rating scales (e.g., 1-5 with one being low and five being high). Run a report showing: "All employees rated '4' or '5' who left voluntarily this year." Analyze their compensation history. Finding that high performers are leaving due to non-competitive pay transforms the review process from an administrative task to a financial risk mitigation tool.

4. **Translate Every Initiative into the Financial Filter.**

   - **Detailed Explanation:** To secure executive approval and funding, all proposals must be presented using the language of the C-Suite: Money and Risk, otherwise known as the Finance Filter. HR jargon must be replaced by one of three financial outcomes.

   - **The Three Financial Categories:**

     - **Increasing Revenue:** Does the program enable a sales team to sell faster or a product team to launch sooner? (e.g., *Proactive hiring for high-demand roles reduces time-to-market for a revenue-generating product.*)

     - **Decreasing Cost:** Does the program reduce an existing company expense? (e.g., *Implementing a predictive hiring model reduces the cost of failed executive hires.*)

     - **Mitigating Risk:** Does the program prevent a future financial or legal liability? (e.g., *A new safety protocol prevents insurance premium hikes.*)

   - **Example:** Frame the proposal as: "We have determined that 70% of our high-performer turnover is driven by poor management. This

$15,000 leadership training program is a risk mitigation strategy that will save the company an estimated $300,000 in annual replacement costs."

5. **Build a Predictive Talent Roadmap.**

    o   **Detailed Explanation:** The ultimate Strategic HR action is moving from *reactive* hiring (filling a seat that's already empty) to *proactive* talent forecasting. This ensures the company is never slowed down by a lack of necessary skills or critical leadership.

The Finance Filter

Translating HR Proposals into Financial Language

Traditional HR Framing	Financial Framing	Executive Benefit (ROI)
Improve morale ➡	Reduce regietable turnovor ➡	Avoid $500K annual cost

    o   **Step-by-Step Action:**

        ▪   **A. Obtain the Roadmap:** Secure the company's product/service or operational roadmap for the next 18-24 months from the relevant executive (CTO, COO). This document defines future skill needs.

        ▪   **B. Conduct a Gap Analysis:** This is a simple equation: Future Demand (What specialized skills will be needed in 18 months?) - Current Supply (What skills are available internally today?) = Critical Gap.

- **C. Implement "Buy" or "Build" Strategy:** If the gap requires external recruitment, implement a Buy strategy (e.g., targeted university partnerships) immediately. If the gap can be closed by internal development, launch a Build (upskilling and training) strategy. Starting this process 18 months early is what defines Strategic HR.

Case Study – short, real-world SMB success snapshot.

A 75-person manufacturing firm invested $12,000 in a simple HRIS with an Employee Self-Service (ESS) function. This reduced the HR Director's time spent on manual timecard auditing and payroll pre-processing from 40% to 5%. The freed capacity was dedicated to building a new safety training program, which led to a 30% reduction in annual OSHA recordable incidents and $60,000 in annual premium savings on workers' compensation insurance.

FORMULA IN ACTION – relevant HR or financial formula with example and explanation.

The Cost of Regrettable Turnover

To effectively communicate the financial risk of talent loss, quantify the cost of replacing a high performer.

Cost of Regrettable Turnover. Departing Employee's Salary X 1.5

- **Example:** If a high-performing senior engineer with a salary of $120,000 leaves due to poor management (a preventable issue), the replacement cost (recruitment, onboarding, lost productivity) is approximately $20,000 X 1.5 = $180,000.

- **Explanation:** The $1.5x multiplier is a conservative estimate that includes the tangible costs of recruiting and training, and the intangible cost of lost productivity while the seat is empty and the new person reaches full efficiency. Strategic HR focuses on avoiding this $180,000 cost.

TIP – actionable professional advice.

Stop Sending Email Attachments. The shift from Tactical to Strategic begins with data consistency. Consolidate all forms, tracking, and communication into a single, centralized HRIS or HCM system. The HR function cannot be strategic if its core data is fragmented across email attachments, spreadsheet tabs, and scattered folders, making pattern analysis impossible.

Common Mistake – a frequent error or misconception to avoid.

Common Mistake

A frequent error is believing that "Employee Happiness is Strategic HR." While employee engagement and happiness are vital, they are outputs of effective management and culture, not the core business goal. The true strategic work is driving business results (Revenue, Cost, Risk) through the human capital asset. Focus on proving that good culture leads to higher sales and lower costs.

Proof: The Strategic Turnaround in Action

The framework outlined above, the shift from administrative cost center to strategic value driver, is not simply a theory. It is a proven, financially viable strategy that transforms the entire perception of Human Resources within the C-Suite.

The Case Study that follows serves a critical dual purpose. First, it is a Proof of Concept. It takes the abstract steps of the Strategic Transition Framework and shows them executed in a real-world, high-stakes environment. You will see Step 1 (Quantify the Administrative Cost) used to secure the budget for automation, followed by Step 4 (The Financial Filter: Mitigating Risk) used to solve a core operational problem that was financially hemorrhaging the company.

Second, the Case Study provides the Template for Executive Buy-In. The outcome is not measured in "forms filed" or "programs completed," but in a direct, quantifiable $150,000 cost saving on the company's insurance premiums. This financial result is the language of the CEO.

You must not read the Case Study as a unique anecdote. Instead, use it as a blueprint: identify the administrative time sinks and the core enterprise risk in your own organization, then follow the same two-phase sequence (Automate the Burden, then Redirect Capacity to Mitigate Risk). The goal is to replicate its outcome: to turn your HR function from a financial drag into a key protector of enterprise value.

Case Study: The Compliance Trap (Manufacturing) The Strategic Turnaround

Issue: The company, a $75 million revenue manufacturing operation, had fallen victim to the Tactical Trap. The HR Director was bogged down, spending an estimated 60% of her week on non-value-added administrative labor: manually auditing thousands of paper timecards, verifying benefits eligibility forms, and maintaining disorganized paper personnel files. This administrative paralysis left no time for proactive risk management. The operational fallout was severe: a chronically high on-the-job injury rate had recently culminated in three major workers' compensation claims within an 18-month period, triggering a non-renewal threat from the insurance carrier and a $150,000 increase in annual premiums. The CEO viewed HR as purely an administrative burden, rather than a solution to the enterprise's financial hemorrhaging (losing a large amount of money rapidly and uncontrollably).

Action: Recognizing that the financial damage was caused by a lack of capacity, the HR Director executed a two-phase strategic shift. First, she conducted a detailed Process-Time-Cost Analysis (Step 1), demonstrating that the manual administrative labor cost the business over $90,000 annually. She used this data to successfully advocate for a simple, cloud-based HRIS with Employee Self-Service (ESS) capabilities. This investment automated the Burden of timecard approval and compliance filing, immediately reducing administrative time by 15%. Second, the newly Redirected Capacity (45% of their time) was immediately focused on the injury problem (Mitigating Risk). The

Director collaborated with Operations to create a data-driven safety protocol, tracking every minor injury by shift, process, and supervisor. This analysis revealed a clear trend: 80% of high-risk injuries occurred early on the second shift, correlating directly with inadequate communication during shift hand-offs and fatigued staff bypassing safety protocols. HR then designed and implemented a mandatory pre-shift safety huddle and a new, standardized machine operation checklist, embedding safety accountability directly into daily operations.

Expected Outcome: The leadership team hoped the intervention would halt the rising injury trend, stabilize the insurance premiums, and prevent further financial exposure.

Actual Outcome: The shift to Strategic HR proved its value quickly. Within one year, the high-risk injury rate dropped dramatically by 40%. Because the company demonstrated proactive risk mitigation, their workers' compensation premiums not only stabilized, but the prior $150,000 increase was successfully reversed in the next insurance renewal cycle (a direct $150,000 cost saving). By moving from managing paperwork to mitigating a core enterprise risk, the HR Director transformed her function from a financial burden to a key protector of enterprise value.

Chapter 1 Checklist

- Have you quantified the cost of time spent on transactional, Administrative HR tasks?

- Do you know your company's #1 goal for the next 12 months, and is your current work aligned with it?

- Have you identified the strategic data that your current Tactical HR programs (like reviews) are failing to analyze?

- Have you calculated a rough estimate of the Cost of Regrettable Turnover for your most expensive role?

- Can you translate your next HR initiative into the language of the C-Suite: Increasing Revenue, Decreasing Cost, or Mitigating Risk?

Key Takeaways

- **The Three Faces:** All HR work falls into three categories: Administrative (Cost Center), Tactical (Program Runner), and Strategic (Value Driver). The goal is to maximize Strategic time.

- **Capacity First:** The first step to becoming strategic is to aggressively automate and outsource Administrative HR work to free up at least 85% of the team's capacity for value-driving initiatives.

- **Activity vs. Impact:** Tactical HR measures activity (e.g., 98% from completion). Strategic HR impact measures outcomes (e.g., how the data from those forms reduced turnover or increased sales).

- **The Financial Filter:** To gain executive buy-in, every HR initiative must be framed using the Finance Filter: does it Increase Revenue, Decrease Cost, or Mitigate Risk?

- **Predictive > Reactive:** Strategic HR uses the company's roadmap to build a Talent Roadmap, ensuring the right skills are available *before* the business needs them, thereby avoiding costly talent deficits.

Reflection

Use these questions to spark discussion with your leadership team.

- What is the estimated dollar cost of the three most time-consuming manual, administrative tasks currently performed by our HR team?

- If we were to track only one business metric (e.g., time-to-market for a new product), how would HR's efforts directly contribute to improving that number?

- What is the biggest future-facing business risk (e.g., skill shortage, leader succession) that HR is currently *not* proactively planning for?

- Can we identify one tactical HR program (like annual reviews) and clearly state the specific business outcome we intend to achieve by analyzing its data?

- What is the #1 business goal for the next 12 months, and what is the single biggest "people problem" that could stop us from achieving it?

Chapter 2: Phase 1: Assess and Clean House (Standardize & Automate)

Summary

Phase 1 focuses on building the foundation for Strategic HR by aggressively tackling the Administrative HR workload. This involves systematically quantifying the cost of manual labor, standardizing core processes, and implementing automation to create essential professional Capacity and secure the clean, reliable data required for strategic analysis.

Step-by-Step Framework

The goal of this phase is clear: If you cannot manage your time, you cannot manage your strategy. The pursuit of a strategic HR function begins not with complex analytics, but with a systematic cleanup of operational clutter. This foundational work, Phase 1: Assess and Clean House, is crucial because the HR professional's greatest asset is time, and every minute spent filing paper or transcribing data is a minute stolen from high-value, profit-driving work. The function must aggressively dismantle the Administrative HR workload by standardizing processes and implementing automation. This focused effort is the only way to convert sunk administrative labor (salary dollars wasted on non-value-added tasks) into the free professional capacity and clean, reliable data that define a true strategic partner.

2.1 The HR Audit: Quantifying the Cost of Inefficiency

Discussion: The HR Audit is the initial, critical operation that distinguishes effective HR leadership from simple program management. Before any costs can be cut or tasks automated, the organization must achieve radical transparency regarding how its HR time is spent. This audit is not a punitive measure; it is an investigation into wasted time for the express purpose of translating that inefficiency into a measurable dollar cost for the business. This cost, known as sunk administrative labor, represents recurring salary expense for work (e.g., manually updating multiple spreadsheets) that yields no competitive advantage. By meticulously quantifying this cost, HR gains the essential financial leverage to prove that the cost of technology is vastly lower than the perpetual, recurring cost of inefficiency.

What It Is: A systematic, meticulous review and cataloging of every process and policy within the HR function. The goal is to create a detailed inventory of all work performed, regardless of its repetitiveness or small scale.

Why It's Important for the Business: The audit provides the hard, data-backed evidence necessary to justify technology investment and prove the ROI (Return on Investment). This allows the business to convert the recurring, non-value-added cost of sunk administrative labor into future profit-driving capacity.

The Strategic Outcome: The audit produces the data required to calculate the true financial burden of current administrative practices, which serves as the foundational financial justification for all subsequent automation and standardization efforts.

Step-by-Step: The Process-Time-Cost Analysis

This is the core financial tool of the HR Audit. It transforms subjective complaints about workload into objective, budgetary demands.

- **Map All Tasks:** Create a granular list of every administrative process the HR team handles. Include seemingly trivial tasks like "manually checking for missing signatures on I-9 forms" or "transcribing paper performance goals into the HCM system." Be comprehensive.

- **Measure Time:** For a defined period (a minimum of two consecutive weeks), staff are to meticulously log the actual time spent on each task. Do not rely on estimates. Cumulative time spent on small tasks (e.g., 15 minutes spent responding to 20 employee emails daily regarding time-off balances) is often the largest financial drain.

- **Identify Bottlenecks:** Pinpoint specific points where manual steps, paper shuffling, or multiple data entries are required. These friction points, where data is hand-copied from one system to another, are not only inefficient but also introduce a high risk of transcription errors, which can lead to costly payroll mistakes or compliance failures.

- **Calculate Cost:** Determine the fully loaded hourly cost for each HR staff member (Base Salary + Cost of Benefits) and multiply this rate by the total annual hours documented for the manual task.

Process-Time-Cost Analysis Template

Optimizing HR Operations

Task	Hours Spent per Year	Horrly Cost	Total Cost	Automation Opportunity (Y/N)
Manual Timecards	1,400 hrs	$35/hr	$49,000	Yes

Formula in Action – The Cost of Sunk Administrative Labor

The core financial metric in Phase 1 is the cost of paying staff to perform non-value-added manual work. This dollar amount is the hard evidence needed to justify the implementation of automation.

Cost of Sunk Administrative Labor = Fully Loaded Hourly Rate x Total Annual Hours Spent on Manual Task.

Example:

- **HR Coordinator Fully Loaded Hourly Rate:** $35 per hour.

- **Manual Task:** Processing paper time-off requests.

- **Total Annual Hours Spent on Task (Audited):** 1,400 hours (as calculated in the Retail Case Study).

Calculation: $35 per hour times 1,400 hours = $49,000

Explanation: The $ 49,000 figure represents the recurring, non-value-added cost of *inaction*. This number proves that spending $ 30,000 once on automation is a financially superior business decision, generating an immediate and permanent labor savings.

Blueprint for Building Capacity: The Case Studies

Phase 1: Assess and Clean House, which involve quantifying the cost of inefficiency and standardizing the process for reliable data.

The first case study, Justifying the HRIS (Retail), shows you exactly how to execute the Process-Time-Cost Analysis to convert hours wasted on paper into a hard, quantified dollar amount. The purpose of reading this case study is to learn how to frame a technology purchase as an investment with guaranteed, rapid ROI to your CFO. You should use the outcome as a model for your own budget proposals.

The second case study, Standardization and Data Reliability (Marketing Agency), shifts the focus from cost reduction to data quality. Its purpose is to demonstrate that a lack of standardized processes is not only frustrating but also actively prevents strategic analysis by creating unreliable, meaningless data. You should use the outcome to counter managerial resistance to process standardization by demonstrating, with irrefutable evidence, how consistent processes lead to a direct reduction in high-cost business problems (like high regrettable turnover).

Case Study: Justifying the HRIS (Retail) The Strategic Turnaround

Issue: A $60 million revenue retail chain struggled with operational overhead due to an entirely paper-based system for time-off requests. The process involved employees filling out physical forms, managers signing them, HR collecting them, manually checking balances, transcribing data into the payroll system, and filing the hard copy. This slow, error-prone workflow was a constant source of friction.

Action Taken (Process-Time-Cost Analysis): The HR Director executed the Process-Time-Cost Analysis with precision. The audit revealed that this single process from receiving the paper form to final filing consumed an average of 7 hours of HR staff time per employee annually. With $200,000 in employee compensation, this represented 1,400 total hours. The calculated labor cost for this single, manual process was a recurring annual cost of $70,000 in sunk administrative labor, which added zero value to sales or operations.

Framed Proposal and Implementation: The Director used the quantified $70,000 annual cost to frame the purchase of a simple $30,000 cloud-based HRIS (Human Resources Information System), not as an expense, but as an investment with a 2-year ROI to the CFO. The argument was simple: "We are paying $70,000 annually to file paper. We can pay $30,000 once to automate it, saving $40,000 in the first year alone." Once approved, the system was implemented, shifting data entry and manager approvals entirely to Employee Self-Service (ESS).

Actual Outcome: The financial justification was irrefutable. By automating this single task, the company immediately eliminated the $70,000 labor cost and, more importantly, generated 1,400 hours of capacity for the HR team. This newly created time was immediately and strategically redirected to analyze causes of inventory shrinkage across different store managers, directly supporting the Operations team's P&L goals.

Automation First Workflow

Optimize HR for Strategic Impact

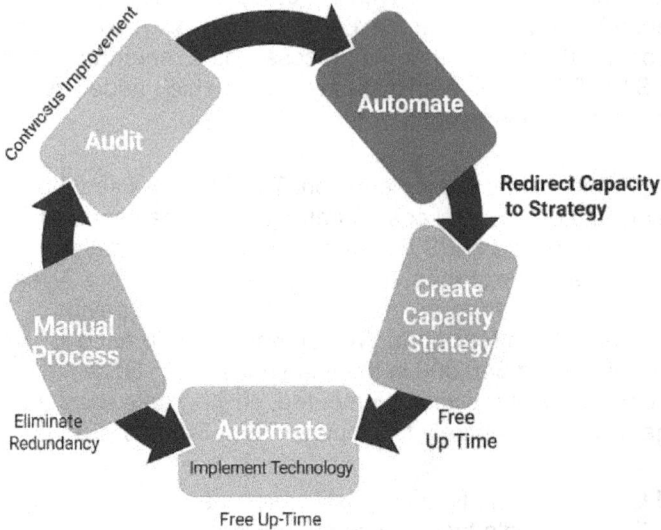

Automation First

The principle of "Automation First" must be a core operational mandate: If a computer can perform a task, a human HR professional should not be responsible for it. This aggressive push for technological delegation is the only way to free up the estimated 30% to 50% of staff time required to engage in high-value strategic initiatives, such as predictive talent planning. This is the act of manufacturing capacity.

Technology Enablement: The HRIS/HCM Foundation

The HRIS (Human Resources Information System) or HCM (Human Capital Management) platform is the technological backbone of a strategic function. This software is not merely a digital filing cabinet for personnel files; it is an enabler of strategy that performs two indispensable tasks: 1) it shifts manual burden away from HR via ESS (Employee Self Service), and 2) it enforces clean, standardized data. Without clean data, all subsequent strategic reports on turnover, performance, and risk are unreliable guesses.

Priority 1: Employee Self-Service (ESS)

ESS is the most powerful tool for capacity creation. It fundamentally shifts the responsibility for routine, personal data entry (e.g., updating addresses, viewing pay stubs, submitting time requests) from HR staff to the employees and managers who own the data. This change drastically reduces administrative workload and virtually eliminates transcription errors, strengthening compliance.

Priority 2: Clean Data Integration and Standardization

Data integrity is the difference between guesswork and actionable insight. The HCM system must be configured to eliminate data inconsistencies at the point of entry.

- **Example: Standardized Coding:** A common error is allowing managers to input free-text reasons for employee departures. A strategically configured HCM system must force managers to select from a standardized, limited list of termination codes (e.g., "Voluntary-Career Advancement," "Involuntary-Performance," "Involuntary-Layoff"). This clean, structured data is essential for Strategic HR to run reliable reports that can accurately diagnose the true causes of turnover.

Communication to the CTO/IT Peer: To secure the necessary budget and technical support, HR must elevate the discussion. Frame the HRIS/HCM platform not as an "HR cost," but as "Critical Data Infrastructure" required for executive-level talent forecasting, risk reporting, and core business intelligence. You are purchasing a system to manage the company's most expensive and valuable asset: its human capital.

2.4 Process Standardization: Ensuring Data Reliability

Discussion: Standardization often meets resistance because it can be perceived as bureaucratic. HR must clearly articulate that the purpose of defining the "one best way" is not rigid rules, but data reliability, which is a core business benefit. If every manager hires differently, the resulting data is a worthless mess of anecdotes. By establishing a single, consistent process for functions like recruiting, onboarding, and performance management, you ensure that every data point generated is comparable across the entire organization. This data reliability allows the executive team to trust HR reports and make smarter, high-confidence strategic investments in talent.

What It Is: Establishing the ideal, standard workflow (the "one best way") for all core HR processes. This ensures consistency in experience and output across the entire company.

Why It's Important for the Business: Standardization ensures that data points are comparable and reliable across the organization. This reliability is the foundation of trustworthy analytics, enabling executives to utilize HR metrics to make informed decisions about resource allocation and risk.

Actionable Steps for Standardization

- **Define:** Establish the ideal, standardized workflow. For recruiting, this means defining the Candidate Interview loop, the mandatory sequence of screenings, interviews, and assessments that every single candidate must clear. This removes managerial subjectivity and enforces a baseline for quality.

- **Document:** Create clear, visual flowcharts and comprehensive checklists that map the "one best way" for all involved parties (HR, hiring managers, and employees). This documentation minimizes tribal knowledge and provides a stable process for training.

- **Train:** Train all managers and stakeholders on the "one best way." Consistently communicate that the strategic reason for adherence is data reliability and fairness, which leads directly to cost reduction and better organizational outcomes.

Case Study: Standardization and Data Reliability (Marketing Agency) The Strategic Turnaround

Impact of Standardization on Turnover
Standardization + Reliability = Lower Turnover

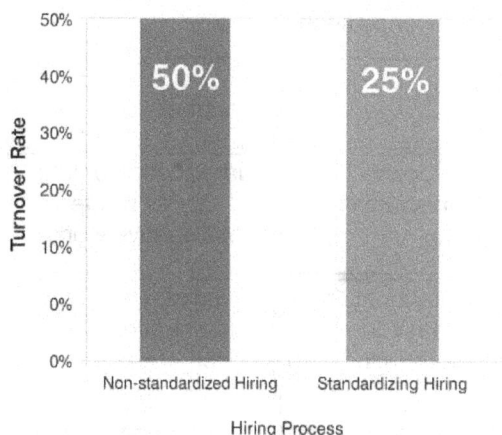

Issue: A $90 million marketing agency was plagued by inconsistent hiring practices across its three key departments (Creative, Account Services, and Technology). One department conducted five rigorous interviews, while another relied on a single informal lunch meeting. As a result, the hiring and retention data was meaningless, preventing leadership from understanding why some teams excelled with new hires while others had constant turnover.

Action Taken (Defining the "One Best Way"): HR led a cross-functional task force to define a single, standard "Candidate Interview Loop" across the entire agency. This loop included mandatory steps, such as a structured behavioral interview and a formal Culture Fit interview designed to assess values and work styles. The HR team rigorously trained all 25 hiring managers on this "one best way," emphasizing that data reliability, not bureaucracy, was the strategic goal. They then configured their new HRIS to track process adherence (whether all steps were completed).

Actual Outcome: The standardized process immediately produced clean, comparable data. Within six months, the HR team conducted a critical analysis, proving that departments with non-standard hiring processes had new hires with a 50% higher regrettable turnover rate within the first year compared to those that strictly followed the standardized process. This data-driven evidence provided an irrefutable business case, not only silencing managerial resistance but also protecting the company from significant recurring replacement and recruitment fees.

Chapter 2 Checklist: Assess and Clean House

Action	Outcome
Action 1: Complete the Process-Time-Cost Analysis for all administrative tasks.	Quantification of time and money wasted on administrative work.
Action 2: Identify the single most time-consuming administrative task for immediate automation/outsourcing (The Quick Win).	Immediate demonstration of capacity creation to the executive team.
Action 3: Document the "one best way" for your two most critical tactical processes (e.g., recruiting and onboarding).	Clean, standardized data for the next phase (Mastering the Data).
Action 4: Frame your technology needs (HRIS/HCM) as "Critical Data Infrastructure" to your IT/Finance peer.	A non-HR-specific justification for your technology budget.

Key Takeaways

- **Time is Capacity:** The first strategic step is converting sunk administrative labor into professional capacity by eliminating manual work.

- **Quantify Inefficiency:** Use the Process-Time-Cost Analysis to translate time wasted on administrative tasks into a measurable dollar cost to justify automation investment.

- **Technology is Strategy:** The HRIS/HCM platform must be viewed as Critical Data Infrastructure that enforces ESS and clean data standards, not just as HR software.

- **Standardization = Reliability:** Define the "one best way" for core processes (like hiring) to ensure data is comparable and reliable across the organization, which enables effective strategic analysis.

Reflection

Use these questions to spark discussion with your leadership team.

- Based on the Process-Time-Cost Analysis, what dollar amount of labor cost could we eliminate by automating the three most inefficient HR tasks?

- If we succeed in freeing up 30% of the HR team's time, what specific, high-cost operational problem (e.g., low sales team productivity, high safety incidents) will we target first with that new capacity?

- Do we currently have standardized termination codes enforced by technology, or is our exit data too disorganized to be reliable for strategic analysis?

- What is the single biggest resistance point to process standardization, and how can we use data reliability as the strategic argument to overcome it?

- How many hours per month do our managers currently spend doing administrative work that could be handled by Employee Self-Service (ESS)?

Chapter 3: Phase 2: Mastering the Data (Metrics & Insights)

Summary

You've successfully built the foundation (Phase 1). Now, Phase 2: Mastering the Data instructs HR on how to utilize clean, reliable data to transition from reporting historical activity to forecasting the future and demonstrating financial impact. This involves adopting core strategic metrics and utilizing data storytelling to align HR initiatives directly with the C-Suite's priorities: money, risk, and growth.

Step-by-Step Framework

With Phase 1: Assess and Clean House complete, the HR function now possesses two crucial assets: professional capacity (time freed from administrative tasks) and clean, reliable data (ensured by standardization and the HRIS). Phase 2: Mastering the Data is the inflection point where HR transcends program management and earns its seat at the executive table. The work in this phase is focused on developing the capability to use data not just to report what happened in the past ("We finished the training"), but to predict the future and fluently speak the language of the executive suite: money, risk, and growth. This is the process of translating complex people activities (such as launching a new training program) into measurable business results (like reduced operational costs or accelerated revenue growth).

3.1 Moving Beyond Headcount: Measuring Impact, Not Effort

Discussion: The biggest and most persistent mistake of a reactive HR function is reporting activity instead of impact. A tactical HR leader reports how busy they were, often citing internal effort: "We conducted 50 interviews!" or "We processed 95% of the performance reviews!" A strategic HR leader reports the tangible business impact of that effort: "Those 50 interviews led to a 10% faster Time-to-Productivity (TTTP) for the sales team, accelerating $50,000 in project revenue." This shift is the definitive differentiator. Your goal must transition from tracking what the HR team did to tracking what happened as a result for the business's bottom line. This means retiring simple metrics like "headcount" (which is merely a census number) and replacing them with metrics that measure efficiency, financial value, and risk.

What It Is: Shifting the core measurement philosophy from focusing on "HR effort" (internal activity metrics) to focusing on "Business Outcomes" (external financial metrics).

Why It's Important for the Business: Executives disregard metrics that only measure internal HR effort. They pay attention only to metrics that directly connect HR's work to their biggest worries: revenue targets, budget control, and growth. This shift in language demonstrates that HR is aligned with the CEO and CFO's priorities.

The Strategic Outcome: The HR team's job transforms from process management (ensuring forms are completed) to consulting and outcome measurement (advising managers on how to strategically use people to achieve business goals).

Stop Saying (Activity/Effort)	Start Saying (Impact/Outcome)
"We conducted 10 performance reviews."	"Turnover dropped 5% in departments that completed the new management training, proving the training's direct impact on a business outcome."
"We offered 15 training hours to the sales team."	"The sales team's average deal size increased by 7% after our new sales coaching program, demonstrating ROI on the training investment."

3.2 The Core Strategic Metrics: The Language of Finance

The Language of Financial HR Metrics

Core Strategic Metrics

Metric	Definition	Business Relevance	Formula Example
Turnover Cost	Total cost of replacing employee	Direct financial impact of churn	Cost of hire
Time-to-Productivitty (TTTP)	Days for a new hire to reach full output	Efficiency of Onboarding/Training	Average Days to Quota / Tenure
Revenue Per Employee	Revenue generated by each FTE	Workforce efficiency & value	Total Revenue Headcount
Talent Forecast Accuracy	Variance between forecast & actuals	Effectiveness of workforce planning	1 – [Actual – Porecast] / Actual

Discussion: To speak the language of the C-Suite (CEO, CFO, COO), the HR function must adopt metrics that are not optional; they are the non-negotiable data points that prove HR is a value driver. These metrics directly quantify the cost or return associated with the human capital asset. They transform vague "people problems" into quantifiable financial problems that compel executive action and secure budgetary approval.

What It Is: Tracking metrics that quantify the cost or return associated with people. These measure the efficiency and financial risk of the workforce.

Why It's Important for the Business: These metrics quantify the financial impact of having the wrong people, losing the right people, or taking too long to integrate new talent. They force leadership to view talent issues not as headaches, but as serious financial drains.

Core Strategic Metric	Detailed Explanation	Strategic Value (Language of the C-Suite)
Turnover Cost	The total financial cost of a lost employee, including separation pay, recruitment fees, interviewer time, training the replacement, and the lost productivity revenue while the position is vacant.	Quantifies poor retention as a measurable financial cost, justifying investment in proactive retention strategies.
Time-to-Productivity (TTTP)	TTTP is the time, measured in weeks or months, from when a new employee starts until they are performing at 90% or more of expected efficiency.	Measures the true quality of recruiting and onboarding, directly linking HR efficiency to revenue acceleration or project speed.
Revenue Per Employee	Calculated simply as: Total Revenue divided by Total Number of Employees	The simplest measure of workforce efficiency. Strategic HR initiatives (e.g., training, process improvement) should aim to increase this number, linking talent quality to overall profitability.

Departmentalizing Revenue Per Employee

The raw company-wide Revenue Per Employee number is useful for benchmarking, but it is often too blunt to drive tactical decisions. To make it a true strategic metric, break it down by department or business unit. Calculating *Sales Revenue Per Sales Employee* or *Revenue Per Engineer* allows you to compare the operational efficiency of different teams. This immediately highlights where strategic HR investments (like specialized training or manager coaching) will yield the highest return on efficiency and profitability.

The Case Studies

The two case studies in this chapter are designed to demonstrate the critical link between data measurement and financial influence.

The first case study, Linking Training to TTTP (Technology), shows you how to establish a financial metric, Time-to-Productivity (TTTP), to prove the value of a traditionally tactical HR program (training/onboarding). The purpose of this case study is to provide a template for demonstrating Return on Investment (ROI). You should use this outcome as a model for quantifying revenue acceleration and justifying an increase in your training budget.

The second case study, Obsolescence Risk (Media), shifts to the predictive power of data. It demonstrates the use of a Talent Forecast (Gap Analysis) to identify a massive, future-facing business risk (skill obsolescence). The purpose is to show how HR transforms from a service function into the chief risk manager for organizational capability. Use this example to integrate your function with your executive team's 3 to 5-year strategic roadmap, thereby securing your role in long-term decision-making.

Case Study: Linking Training to TTTP (Technology) The Strategic Turnaround

Issue: An HR team at a $120 million tech firm discovered, through an internal operational audit, that new software engineers took an average of 14 weeks (over three months) to reach 90% project efficiency (TTTP). This 14-week ramp-up was wasting significant salary costs and delaying the revenue recognition from client projects.

Action Taken (Data-Driven Intervention):

- **Calculated TTTP Baseline:** HR established the 14-week TTTP metric as the baseline measure of onboarding failure.

- **Designed Intervention:** They revamped the tactical onboarding program, including mandatory, intensive, specialized training on proprietary coding standards and cross-functional collaboration tools.

- **Measured Impact:** HR tracked the TTTP for the next three cohorts of new hires post-intervention.

- **Calculated ROI:** They translated the reduction into a financial return using Data Storytelling.

Actual Outcome: TTTP dropped from 14 weeks to a significantly improved 10 weeks. This four-week reduction resulted in four weeks of salary saved and, more importantly, four weeks of accelerated project revenue for every new engineer hired. HR presented the data: "Reducing TTTP by four weeks on 20 hires this year accelerated project completion by 80 collective weeks, translating to $150,000 in recognized revenue this quarter." This proved the training's impact on a core business outcome (revenue acceleration), justifying continued, increased investment in the development program.

3.3 Data Storytelling: The Art of Influence

Discussion: Having perfect data is meaningless if you present it as a complicated, dense spreadsheet. Executives will ignore it. The critical skill of Strategic HR is Data Storytelling, the ability to translate complex HR metrics into a clear, compelling business narrative. Data storytelling connects your HR metric (a number, such as turnover rate) to the company's biggest pain point (a financial drain, like missed revenue, or an operational risk, like project delays). This is the final step that turns raw information into actionable influence, securing funding and executive approval for your strategic proposals.

What It Is: Translating HR metrics (e.g., turnover rate or cycle time) into direct financial consequences (e.g., project delays, missed revenue, or increased operational risk).

Why It's Important for the Business: This approach reframes HR as a function that proactively identifies and addresses the company's most significant challenges. It secures approval and funding because the proposal is not about "better HR," but about "better money management."

Actionable Steps: The Data Story and Proposal Flow

The Data Storystelling Flow
Crafting HR Narratives for Executive Buy-in

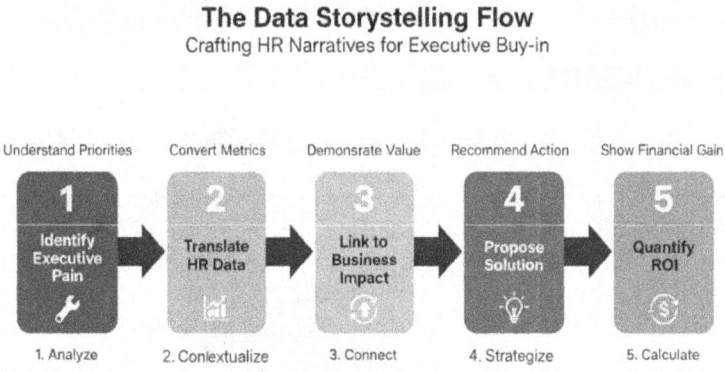

Understand Priorities	Convert Metrics	Demonsrate Value	Recommend Action	Show Financial Gain
1 Identify Executive Pain	**2** Translate HR Data	**3** Link to Business Impact	**4** Propose Solution	**5** Quantify ROI
1. Analyze	2. Conlextualize	3. Connect	4. Strategize	5. Calculate

The following sequence moves the conversation from simply identifying a problem to presenting a financially justified solution, ensuring the executive team is compelled to act.

Data Story Flow	Step in the Executive Conversation	Description	Example
1. Identify Executive Pain	The Target	Determine the current financial target, operational deadline, or risk the executive is	"We are worried about missing our Q4 revenue target."

Data Story Flow	Step in the Executive Conversation	Description	Example
		most worried about.	
2. Translate HR Data to Dollars	The Proof (The Cost)	Convert a specific HR metric into a financial cost related to that pain point.	"Our recruiting cycle time increased by 10 days last quarter."
3. Link to Business Impact	The Story	Tie the data directly to the executive's concern (dollars, risk, or strategic deadlines) using strong, direct language.	"The 10-day increase in our recruiting cycle time delayed the critical Alpha Project launch by 2 weeks, resulting in a $50,000 loss of projected Q4 revenue."
4. Propose the Solution	The Action	Define the specific, focused initiative that will reverse the negative financial trend.	"We propose a $15,000 investment in standardized interview software and manager training to streamline candidate review."
5. Quantify the Return	The Payoff (The ROI)	Clearly state the projected financial benefit of the solution.	"This will cut the cycle time by 15 days, saving the company an estimated $75,000 on future project

Data Story Flow	Step in the Executive Conversation	Description	Example
			acceleration over the next year."

3.4 Building the Talent Forecast: Predicting Future Needs

Discussion: The Talent Forecast is the ultimate predictive function of Strategic HR. It shifts the entire organization from reacting to current job openings to proactively ensuring the company has the right people with the right skills at the right time in the future. This requires HR to integrate deeply with the executive team's 3 to 5-year strategic plan. By providing this foresight, HR transforms its role from a reactive service provider into the chief risk manager for talent, guaranteeing the company's ability to execute its long-term goals.

What It Is: A Gap Analysis that systematically compares the future skills the business will require (Demand) against the skills the current workforce possesses (Supply).

Why It's Important for the Business: It prevents the devastating Talent Deficit trap (as described in Chapter 1) by giving the company years of lead time to recruit, re-skill, or train for critical future capabilities. Without this, the business will be forced to panic-hire at extreme cost when a new technology is suddenly needed.

Preparation: The HR team must obtain the 3–5-year product roadmap, technology adoption plans, and market expansion goals directly from the executive team.

Actionable Steps: The Gap Analysis

Talent Forecast Gap Analysis
Projected Skill Demand vs. Current Supply

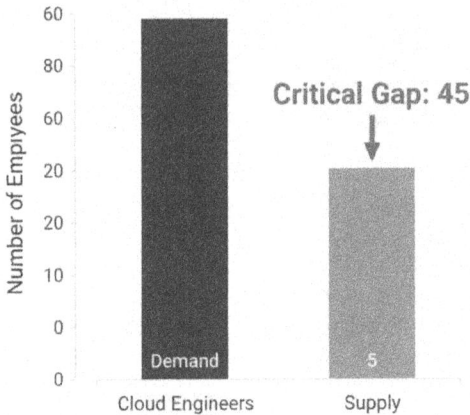

- **Model Future Demand (The "How"):** This number is determined by translating the business's long-term strategic plan into specific talent requirements.

  o **Obtain the Strategic Plan:** Secure the 3–5-year roadmap.

  o **Deconstruct the Initiative:** Ask functional leaders (e.g., the CTO): "What specific, new technology or product capability is required to achieve this goal?"

  o **Determine the Volume (The Demand Number):** Ask the functional leader: "How many full-time people with this new skill (e.g., specialized cloud architecture) are needed to run the project or maintain the new technology?" This translates a technical requirement into a quantifiable headcount number.

- **Audit Current Supply:** Assess the current workforce's skills and capacity relative to the demand number. This is often accomplished through a simple internal skills audit, leveraging manager feedback and structured employee self-assessments within your HRIS.

- **Identify Critical Gaps:** Pinpoint the delta (difference) between future demand and current supply (e.g., "We need 50 specialized roles, we currently have 5"). This 45-person deficit is the Critical Gap.

- **Proactive Closure:** Immediately launch either a Build strategy (internal re-skilling programs) or a Buy strategy (targeted, long-lead-time recruiting programs) to close the gap before the business needs the talent.

Case Study: Obsolescence Risk (Media) The Strategic Turnaround

Issue: An $80 million media company's 3-year strategic plan hinged on a major technological shift to new cloud-based video editing software to launch a new streaming service. The current workforce's skills were entirely tied to obsolete desktop software, creating a critical Skill Gap and enormous future operational risk that threatened the entire project timeline.

Action Taken (Gap Analysis and Proactive Closure):

- **Modeled Future Demand (The Translation):** HR met with the VP of Production and determined that to launch the streaming service on time, 70% of the 50 video editors (35 people) would need certification in the new cloud editing software. This was the demand number.

- **Audited Current Supply:** HR used an internal skills audit to confirm that only 2 editors had experience with the new software.

- **Identified Critical Gap:** The difference was 33 editors; a massive Skill Gap that could delay the new service by a year.

- **Proactive Closure:** Recognizing they couldn't hire 33 specialized editors instantly, they immediately launched a mandatory, incentivized upskilling program (the Build talent strategy). They partnered with a training vendor and offered paid time for certification completion.

Actual Outcome: The HR team successfully closed the skill gap on time, allowing the company to launch the new streaming service without delay. This proactive action avoided a major operational bottleneck and the costly, panicked external hiring that would have occurred. The HR team was successfully positioned as the chief manager of Adaptability Risk.

Chapter 3 Checklist: Mastering the Data

Action	Outcome
Action 1: Calculate your current Turnover Cost and Time-to-Productivity (TTTP) baseline metrics.	The first two core strategic metrics for measuring financial impact.
Action 2: Conduct a preliminary Talent Forecast (Gap Analysis) for one critical department over the next 3 years.	Pinpoints the biggest future talent risk (the "Critical Gaps").
Action 3: Draft a complete "Data Story" translating your turnover cost into a consequence linked to a current or recent organizational failure (e.g., project delay, missed revenue target).	The capability to speak the language of the C-Suite and predict future talent risk.

Key Takeaways

- **Shift from Effort to Impact:** Replace internal "activity" reporting (e.g., forms processed) with external "outcome" reporting (e.g., revenue acceleration, cost reduction).

- **Quantify the Cost of Talent:** Utilize Core Strategic Metrics like Turnover Cost and Time-to-Productivity to translate people problems into quantifiable financial consequences.

- **Master Data Storytelling:** The ability to connect an HR metric to a financial consequence (e.g., turnover to missed Q4 revenue) is the critical skill that secures executive influence and funding.

- **Be Predictive:** Use the Talent Forecast (Gap Analysis) to proactively identify future skill deficits, transforming

HR into the chief manager of organizational risk and long-term capability.

Reflection

Use these questions to spark discussion with your leadership team.

- What is the current TTTP for our most expensive or revenue-critical role, and what is the estimated financial cost of that ramp-up time?

- Based on our company's 3-year plan, what new technology or market goal will create our biggest future Skill Gap, and what is our current lead time to recruit or train for it?

- What is the most financially damaging business failure (e.g., project delay, regulatory fine) we experienced in the last year, and how could a Strategic HR metric have predicted or prevented it?

- How can we redesign one core tactical program (e.g., a mandatory training) to measure its impact on a financial metric (e.g., error rate, sales volume) instead of just attendance?

Chapter 4: Phase 3: Building the Strategic Portfolio

Summary: Phase 3 - Building the Strategic Portfolio

Phase 3 transitions the HR function from internal data generation (Phase 2) to designing and executing long-term, external talent systems that directly sustain business growth and competitive advantage. The focus is on leveraging data insights and professional capacity to establish HR as a strategic guarantor of the organization's future success, shifting its perception from overhead to essential investment.

Key Components and Outcomes

Component	Description	Strategic Outcome
Alignment Workshop	A mandatory session to formally link the corporate 3-year strategic plan directly to HR priorities and investments.	**Formal Validation:** Secures executive sign-off, ensuring the entire HR budget is viewed as a justified investment in business goals.
Talent Strategy	The multi-year (3-5 year) blueprint for sourcing, developing, and retaining the skills needed for future success, focusing on Critical Roles.	**Proactive Mitigation:** Mitigates the financial risk of skill shortages using the most cost-effective and sustainable sourcing approach (Buy, Build, or Borrow).

Component	Description	Strategic Outcome
Culture Blueprint	Defines the specific values and behaviors (e.g., risk-taking, fast decision-making) that must be explicitly rewarded and enforced to enable the business strategy.	**Competitive Moat:** a unique structural advantage that protects its long-term profits and market share from competitors, Ensures internal behaviors reinforce external goals, preventing strategy failure due to cultural misalignment.
Succession Readiness Score (SRS)	A quantifiable metric that measures the company's vulnerability to the loss of critical leaders (Talent Risk).	**Risk Mitigation:** Transforms HR into the chief manager of Organizational Health Risk, forcing executive action and funding for targeted development.

Phase 3 marks the organization's shift from internal data generation (Phase 2) to designing external, long-term talent systems that directly sustain business growth and competitive advantage. This involves formally validating HR priorities through an Alignment Workshop, creating the Talent Strategy (Buy, Build, Borrow), and actively managing Organizational Health Risk via metrics like the Succession Readiness Score.

Step-by-Step Framework

With the successful completion of Phase 1 (Capacity creation) and Phase 2 (Data capability establishment), the HR function is no longer merely reacting to problems; it now possesses the necessary time and the quantified metrics to exert true influence.

Phase 3: Building the Strategic Portfolio is the culmination of this foundational work. The focus transitions entirely to designing and executing external, long-term talent systems that directly secure business longevity and competitive advantage. This involves leveraging the newly gained professional capacity and data insights to develop formalized, multi-year human capital strategies. This deliberate action earns HR the highest level of credibility by proving the function is integral to achieving the organization's financial and market objectives, transforming the perception from overhead expense to strategic guarantor of future success.

4.1 Alignment Workshop: Formalizing the Strategic Co-Pilot Role

The Alignment Workshop is the single most critical governance mechanism for formalizing HR's role as a strategic co-pilot to the executive team. Historically, HR initiatives, such as creating a new management training program, were often perceived as isolated administrative projects disconnected from the CEO's concerns. This workshop dispels that perception by requiring the HR function to formally align its priorities with the company's 3-5 highest-level, multi-year objectives. By facilitating this structured session and securing executive endorsement on these direct linkages, HR ensures that every subsequent investment in talent from training budgets to recruiting pipeline capacity is 100% justified by its direct contribution to a CEO- or Board-established business goal. This process is foundational because it ensures the entire HR budget is always viewed as an investment in achieving business goals, thereby securing its protection from cost-cutting measures.

What It Is: A formal, structured, and mandatory working session with the executive team dedicated to explicitly linking the corporate 3-year strategic plan directly to the human capital priorities that enable its execution.

Why It's Important for the Business: This mechanism directs the entire HR budget toward strategies that have been formally validated by the C-Suite, ensuring maximum Return on Investment (ROI) for every people-related expenditure. It eliminates the risk of HR resources being wasted on projects that don't matter to the bottom line.

The Strategic Outcome: The documented HR strategy is now formally validated as the function that ensures the organization has the necessary people capacity (skills, leadership, and numbers) to achieve its business goals.

Step-by-Step Action: Hosting the Alignment Workshop

Alignment Workshop Mapping
Connecting HR Strategy to Business Goals

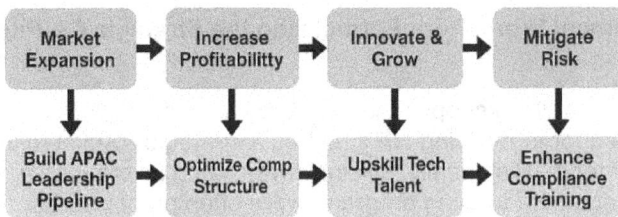

Market Expansion	→	Increase Profitabilitty	→	Innovate & Grow	→	Mitigate Risk
↓		↓		↓		↓
Build APAC Leadership Pipeline	→	Optimize Comp Structure	→	Upskill Tech Talent	→	Enhance Compliance Training

- **Preparation (Summarize Goals):** The HR leader must consult the annual report, board documents, and executive strategy presentations to distill the company's 3-year strategic plan into 3-5 clear, measurable core business goals (e.g., "Grow market share in APAC by 20%," "Reduce Cost of Goods Sold by 5%," or "Launch new Gen AI platform in 30 months").

- **Workshop Goal (Map Priorities):** Facilitate the formal mapping session. For each core business goal, the HR leader must articulate and obtain executive agreement on the 1-2 corresponding HR priorities required to achieve it.

  - *Example:* If the business goal is "Grow market share in APAC (Asia Pacific) by 2%" the HR leader presents the required capacity: "To meet this, we need a talent pipeline fluent in local regulations, languages, and capable of operating within specific foreign sales channels." The resulting HR priority is: "Establish the APAC talent pipeline and local leadership development plan."

- **Conclusion (Formal Validation):** Create a final, concise document that clearly maps the Business Goal to Required Talent Capacity to HR Investment. The CEO must formally sign off on this document. This document serves as the HR function's constitutional mandate, confirming that the HR strategy is formally validated and that the function ensures the organization possesses the people capacity required to achieve its business goals.

4.2 The Talent Strategy: The Buy, Build, or Borrow Decision

Buy-Build-Borrow Decision Matrix
Talent Strategy Comparison

Strategy	Speed	Cost	Cost	Risk	Knowledge Retention
Buy	High	High	Moderate	Risk	Low
Build	Medium	Medium	Low	High	High
Borrow	High	Variable	High	High	None

Discussion: The Talent Strategy is the multi-year (3-5 year) blueprint for the workforce. It leverages the predictive data from the Talent Forecast (Chapter 3), identifies skill gaps, and translates them into a concrete, cost-effective action plan for securing future capabilities. This strategy requires identifying Critical Roles, those 5-10 positions that are absolutely essential for future success, and concentrating the majority of development and retention investment on them, rather than wasting resources by distributing them evenly across all roles. The most sophisticated element is the Buy, Build, or Borrow decision, which determines the single most cost-effective, risk-aware, and sustainable sourcing method for closing each identified future skill gap.

What It Is: A 3–5-year blueprint defining exactly how the company will source, develop, and retain the skills necessary to fulfill future business goals.

Why It's Important for the Business: It proactively mitigates the financial risk of a sudden skill shortage (Talent Deficit) and ensures that all resource allocation is strategically focused on the roles that will generate the highest value for the company's future growth.

Buy, Build, or Borrow: Defining the Sourcing Strategy

This framework outlines the strategic approach for addressing the skill gaps identified in the Talent Forecast, striking a balance between speed, cost, and risk.

- **Buy (Recruit Externally):** Best for immediate, high-demand, highly specialized skills (e.g., a seasoned Data Scientist). This is the fastest, but often the most expensive option, and carries the highest risk of poor culture fit. Use for skills needed immediately.

- **Build (Develop Internally):** Best for skills where company-specific knowledge is required (e.g., leadership roles or custom-technology expertise). This option is generally more cost-effective, fosters employee loyalty, and leverages existing organizational knowledge, but requires a significant amount of time (often 12 months) and an upfront investment in training programs. Use for skills needed in the future.

- **Borrow (Source Temporarily):** Best for short-term projects, sudden peak workloads, or highly specific technical tasks. This utilizes consultants or contractors. It offers flexibility but does not build long-term internal capability or knowledge retention. Use for bridging temporary capacity gaps.

Blueprint for Long-Term Strategy: The Case Studies

The two case studies in this chapter are designed to demonstrate the critical practices required to secure your organization's future capability and manage its leadership risk.

The first case study, "Buy, Build, or Borrow (Construction Tech)," demonstrates the financial and strategic advantages of adopting a mixed approach over a straightforward "Buy" strategy for talent acquisition. The purpose of this case study is to provide a template for creating a cost-effective, sustainable Talent Strategy that balances immediate needs with long-term cost reduction. You should use the outcome to justify a blended approach to your CFO, proving that internal development (Build) saves money and boosts retention.

The second case study, Succession Readiness Score (Pharmaceutical), focuses on the highest level of Risk Mitigation. Its purpose is to show how to quantify a previously abstract threat (leadership loss) into a mandatory business metric that drives executive action. You should use the outcome as a model to create and report your own Succession Readiness Score, transforming HR into the chief manager of Organizational Health Risk and securing funding for development and retention of your next generation of leaders.

Case Study: Buy, Build, or Borrow (Construction Tech) The Strategic Turnaround

Issue: A $40 million construction tech startup's 3-year plan required the hiring of 15 specialized Data Visualization Engineers to manage sensor data from construction sites. The Talent Forecast confirmed a Critical Gap of 15 roles. The external market was highly competitive and expensive, with average salaries 25% higher than the company's budget, making an all-external hiring approach (Buy) financially unsustainable.

Action Taken (Strategic Sourcing Mix): HR applied a balanced strategy guided by the Talent Strategy blueprint.

- **Applied "Buy" Strategy:** They budgeted for and immediately recruited 5 experienced Engineers (Buy) at a premium. This was necessary for speed, allowing the core project to launch and establishing an internal mentorship base.

- **Applied "Build" Strategy:** They assessed 10 high-potential internal software engineers whose skills were foundational but needed specialization. HR created a rigorous, 18-month internal development and mentorship program to convert them into Data Visualization Engineers (Build). This secured a sustainable pipeline at a lower long-term cost, leveraging internal domain knowledge.

- **Applied "Borrow" Strategy:** They strategically utilized two short-term consultants (Borrow) on 6-month contracts to manage the initial workload during the 18-month transition phase, effectively bridging the capacity gap until the internal "Build" team was fully competent.

Actual Outcome: This balanced approach reduced the overall hiring and talent acquisition cost by approximately 30% compared to an all-"Buy" approach over the three-year period. Furthermore, by providing a clear internal development path to 10 existing high-potential employees, the company simultaneously reduced the regrettable turnover rate among its existing high performers by 15%, thereby transforming the Talent Strategy into a dual measure of cost reduction and retention.

4.3 The Culture Blueprint: A Competitive Moat

Discussion: The Culture Blueprint elevates culture from a descriptive concept ("how we feel here") to a strategic, designed business tool. Culture is simply the collective way work gets done within the organization. Strategic HR defines the specific values and behaviors that must be explicitly rewarded and enforced to enable the business strategy. For example, if the business goal is rapid market entry and innovation, the Culture Blueprint must explicitly reward and measure Fast Decision-Making and Calculated Risk-Taking. Conversely, if the culture rewards only caution and consensus (a typical trait of an established company), the innovation strategy will inevitably fail, regardless of the quality of the people. By actively designing and enforcing the culture through all people systems (rewards, performance management, recognition), HR ensures internal behaviors reinforce strategic goals, turning culture into a valuable and difficult-to-copy competitive moat.

What It Is: A defined plan outlining the specific values, beliefs, and behaviors that are necessary to successfully execute the company's core business strategy.

Why It's Important for the Business: It ensures the company's internal behaviors align precisely with its external goals. A misaligned culture is the single most common reason a solid business strategy (e.g., "be the market disruptor") fails to launch.

Succession Readiness Heat Map
Visualizing Future Leadership

	Readiness Level	Ready in 1–2 Years	No Successor
Key Leadership Roles		Ready in 1–2 Years	
CEO			
VP Marketing			
CTO	CTO		
CFO	CFO		
Head of Sales			No
HR Director			

Green = Ready Now
Yellow = 1–2 Years

Discussion: Strategic HR owns organizational health risk, acting as the chief protector of enterprise value. The function operates as a proactive early warning system by actively identifying and measuring "people risks" before they lead to catastrophic financial or operational failure. This requires the formal tracking and reporting of metrics such as the Succession Readiness Score to the executive team, which quantifies the company's vulnerability to leadership loss. The unexpected departure of a CEO, VP of Sales, or Chief Architect can cripple a business for over a year, imposing staggering replacement costs and lost revenue. This proactive reporting elevates HR beyond administrative duties, positioning the function as a key protector of the company's stability and future valuation.

What It Is: Proactively identifying, measuring, and reporting on organizational weaknesses (Talent Risk, Capacity Risk, Internal Climate Risk) before they cause financial damage or operational failure.

Why It's Important for the Business: Strategic HR acts as the chief talent risk manager, providing the executive team with the foresight necessary to manage threats that can suddenly cripple operations, such as the unexpected departure of a critical leader.

Action Detail: Creating the Succession Readiness Score

The Succession Readiness Score is a simple, quantifiable metric that reports to the executive team exactly how vulnerable the company is to losing a key leader. This score directly measures Talent Risk.

- **Identify Critical Roles:** List the 5-10 roles that would cause the most severe operational or financial harm to the business if left vacant for six months (e.g., CEO, VP of Sales, Chief Architect, Head of Regulatory Compliance).

- **Assess Pipeline:** For each role, the HR Business Partner assesses the internal talent pipeline by assigning a numerical readiness score to the top internal candidate:

    - 0 = No candidate identified. (Highest Risk: Immediate crisis if incumbent leaves.)

    - 1 = Candidate identified, needs significant development (18+ months). (Medium-High Risk)

    - 2 = Candidate identified, ready in 6-12 months. (Low Risk)

    - 3 = Candidate is immediately ready. (No Risk)

- **Calculate the Score:** Sum the individual scores for all critical roles and divide by the maximum possible score (Number of Roles times).

- o *Example:* 5 Critical Roles. Total score (sum of readiness) 8. Max Score 5 = 15. Succession Readiness Score 8/15 = 53%.

- **Report to Executive Scorecard:** Report the percentage (53%) directly to the executive team. Presenting this clear vulnerability percentage forces management to acknowledge the gap (the 47% risk) and fund targeted development programs to increase the required readiness percentage, making the Talent Risk immediately quantifiable and actionable.

Common Mistake – Planning Around People, Not Roles

A tactical approach to succession planning focuses on the *person* ("Who will replace Jane?"). A strategic approach focuses on the *role* ("What capabilities are required for the VP of Sales role in 3 years?"). Never build a succession plan around the specific personality or skills of the *current* incumbent. Instead, define the future capabilities the role will require to execute the strategy (e.g., global expansion, AI integration) and then assess candidates against those future-focused needs.

Case Study: Succession Readiness Score (Pharmaceutical Sector) The Strategic Turnaround

I. Context: The Challenge of Incumbent-Focused Planning

A. Organization Profile

A mid-sized, publicly traded pharmaceutical company specializing in complex biologics and niche therapeutic areas was facing a critical juncture: the patents on two of its flagship products were set to expire in three to five years. This required a radical, immediate strategic pivot toward AI-driven drug discovery, as well as accelerated global market penetration in emerging markets.

B. The Common Mistake in Action

The company's prior succession planning model was notoriously incumbent-centric, mirroring the "Planning Around People, Not

Roles" mistake. For years, the leadership team's succession discussions focused on finding an internal candidate who could exactly replicate the outgoing leader's methods, resulting in a talent pipeline filled with "mini-me" candidates. These individuals were trained to execute the incumbent's past success, rather than drive the organization's future strategy. This approach created a leadership capability gap that threatened the upcoming strategic pivot.

Key Role	Incumbent's Primary Skillset (Past Focus)	Future Role Capability Needs (Strategic Focus)
SVP, Research & Development	Deep expertise in legacy small-molecule chemistry.	**AI/ML integration** for target identification, data governance, and open innovation models.
VP, Global Sales	Strong regional US network; Traditional physician detailing models.	**Digital omnichannel marketing**, emerging market regulatory expertise, and value-based pricing strategies.
Chief Operating Officer (COO)	Mastery of existing in-house manufacturing and supply chain.	Global third-party manufacturing oversight; Supply chain resilience via advanced analytics; M&A integration leadership.

II. **The Strategic Solution**: Implementing the Succession Readiness Score (SRS)

To correct the course and decouple succession from existing individuals, the company introduced a strategic, role-focused succession framework anchored by the Succession Readiness Score (SRS).

A. Defining Future-Focused Role Capabilities

The first step was to define the Future Capability Profile (FCP) for 15 critical executive roles, projecting the necessary skills three to five years out. These FCPs were directly tied to the global expansion and AI integration strategy.

- **Example: FCP for SVP, R&D:** Required capabilities included "Familiarity with foundational AI/ML models," "Ability to lead cross-functional data science teams," and "Experience launching biologics in at least two Asian markets."

B. The Succession Readiness Score (SRS) Methodology

The SRS was calculated for each potential candidate for a critical role using a weighted, objective methodology:

SRS = (0.50) times Future Capability Alignment + (0.30 times Development Plan Progress + (0.20 times Organizational Impact/Potential)

Component	Weight	Assessment Metric
Future Capability Alignment	50%	Candidate assessment against the FCP (not the incumbent's current skills).
Development Plan Progress	30%	The rigor and completion rate of personalized, strategy-aligned development actions (e.g., external AI certification, international secondment).
Organizational Impact/Potential	20%	C-suite assessment of the candidate's executive presence

Component	Weight	Assessment Metric
		and potential for broader company leadership.

III. Execution and Results

A. The Case of the VP, Global Sales Role

When the SRS was initially run, the long-standing "heir apparent" for the VP of Global Sales, a top US sales performer, received a low SRS of 45/100. While his current performance was excellent, his Future Capability Alignment score was poor due to a lack of experience in digital marketing and emerging markets.

The analysis highlighted a high-potential regional director from a smaller division who was previously overlooked. Her initial SRS was 75/100. She already possessed strong analytical skills and had led a digital transformation pilot, aligning closely with the Future Capability Profile.

Candidate Profile	Previous Assumption	Initial SRS	Key Gap/Strength	Action Taken
Incumbent Favorite	Ready to take over.	45	**Gap:** Zero digital or emerging market experience.	Moved to a high-impact, short-term role focused on maximizing current portfolio revenue. No longer the heir.
Strategic Candidate	Needs more "seasoning."	75	**Strength:** High Future	Elevated to a 12-month

Candidate Profile	Previous Assumption	Initial SRS	Key Gap/Strength	Action Taken
			Capability Alignment; experience in digital pilot.	assignment leading a critical Asia-Pacific Market Strategy initiative to close her gap.

B. Strategic Outcomes

Within two years of implementing the SRS framework:

- **Talent Pool Quality Improved (40\):** The average SRS for the top-two candidates in the critical roles increased by 40%, indicating a much higher alignment with the future strategic needs (e.g., from an average of 48 to 67).

- **Successful Strategic Hires:** The Strategic Candidate was successfully appointed as the new VP, Global Sales. She immediately launched the company's first omnichannel digital marketing campaign, leading to a 15% faster market penetration in critical emerging economies than initially projected.

- **Enhanced Development Investment:** Development budgets shifted away from generic training to targeted, high-impact activities (e.g., strategic secondments, executive coaching on AI ethics), ensuring development spending was directly linked to future strategy execution.

- **Reduced Transition Risk:** The new framework ensured that when the SVP of R&D retired, the successor was chosen not for their familiarity with the old process, but for their proven readiness to integrate AI/ML; a capability now deemed essential for the company's long-term survival.

IV. **Conclusion**: The Power of Strategic Alignment

By shifting its focus from "Who is like the person leaving?" to "What capabilities must the role have to execute the strategy?" and quantifying this readiness through the Succession Readiness Score, the organization successfully broke the cycle of incumbent-driven planning.

The SRS provided an objective, data-driven mechanism to ensure that the individuals being groomed for top roles were the ones best equipped to lead the organization into its complex and high-stakes future. This strategic turnaround positioned the company to successfully navigate its patent cliff and embrace disruptive technologies.

Chapter 4 Checklist: Building the Strategic Portfolio

Action	Outcome
Action 1: Schedule the Alignment Workshop with the executive team.	Formal validation of the HR strategy as the enabler of business goals.
Action 2: Finalize the Talent Strategy by assigning "Buy, Build, or Borrow" strategies to your top three critical roles.	A defensible, multi-year plan for talent sourcing that balances cost and risk.
Action 3: Define 2-3 specific cultural behaviors that enable the company's current business strategy.	Ensures your culture actively supports, rather than passively tolerates, the business plan.
Action 4: Create a preliminary Succession Readiness Score for the top five leaders in the company.	Proactive identification and quantification of your most immediate Talent Risk.

Key Takeaways

- **Formal Validation is Key:** The Alignment Workshop must formally link every HR investment to a specific, executive-approved business goal, protecting the HR budget.

- **Talent as a Strategy:** The Talent Strategy uses a Buy, Build, or Borrow framework to ensure the most cost-effective, sustainable sourcing method is used to close skill gaps.

- **Culture Must Be Designed:** Culture must be proactively designed to enforce the behaviors (e.g., risk-taking, collaboration) required by the strategic business plan.

- **Quantify Leadership Risk:** The Succession Readiness Score provides the executive team with a simple, quantifiable metric of the company's vulnerability to losing critical leaders, forcing proactive development funding.

Reflection

Use these questions to spark discussion with your leadership team.

- If our top-performing leader in our most critical role resigned tomorrow, what is the estimated dollar cost of the resulting operational disruption and replacement?

- What is one cultural behavior currently rewarded (e.g., caution, consensus-seeking) that actively undermines our 3-year business strategy (e.g., rapid innovation)?

- Of the 3-5 core business goals defined by the CEO, which single goal is currently most at risk due to a lack of required talent capacity?

- Do we need to Buy (pay a premium for), Build (train internally), or Borrow (use a consultant for) the specialized talent needed for our next major product launch?

- What is the target Succession Readiness Score percentage we must achieve by the end of the fiscal year, and what development programs must be funded to get there?

Chapter 5: Speaking the Language of the C-Suite

Summary

The greatest barrier to becoming a Strategic HR leader is language; credibility hinges on translating every proposal into the terminology of the P&L (Profit and Loss) statement. This chapter provides the framework, the Finance Filter, and the communication strategy to quantify the financial impact of HR initiatives, positioning the function as a strategic partner focused on Cost, Revenue, and Risk management.

Step-by-Step Framework

The primary obstacle keeping HR professionals from being seen as true business leaders is the way they communicate. Senior executives make decisions based on financial performance, company valuation, and risk exposure. They expect every recommendation to connect clearly to those measures. They are less interested in terms like morale, satisfaction, or engagement by themselves, as those concepts only gain attention when they are tied directly to measurable results, such as cost savings, stronger revenue, or reduced liability. To be recognized as a strategic contributor rather than an administrative support function, HR must present its work in financial terms and show how each effort affects the bottom line. This chapter equips you with the language, structure, and communication methods needed to speak to decision-makers in the terms they rely on.

5.1 The Finance Filter: Cost, Revenue, and Risk

The Finance Filter Framework

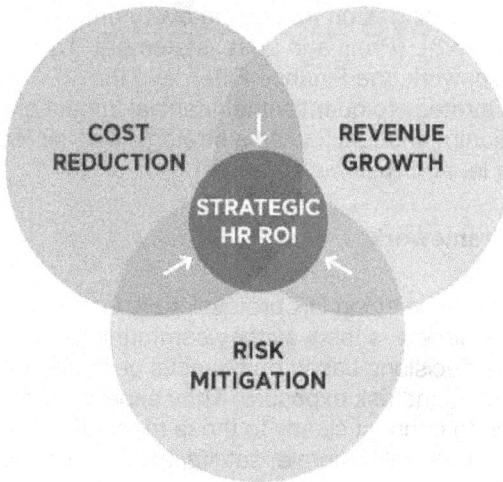

Discussion: The Finance Filter is the core operational principle for all strategic HR communication. It compels the HR function to screen every proposal through the executive team's three primary objectives: increasing revenue, decreasing costs, or managing risk. Executives are stewards of the firm's financial health and market position. They inherently view HR programs as discretionary overhead until those programs are explicitly proven otherwise. Therefore, the strategic task is to translate HR concepts (e.g., "improving employee satisfaction") into financial results (e.g., "reducing regrettable turnover and replacement costs"). By meticulously quantifying an initiative's effect on one of these three levers, HR elevates the conversation from an internal function's request for resources to a budgetary solution for a recognized. This shift in framing is what secures buy-in and funding.

What It Is: A mandatory communication framework requiring every HR initiative to justify its existence based on its measurable, quantifiable effect on the company's financial health.

Why It's Important for the Business: It enforces a discipline that ensures HR resources are only invested in programs that deliver tangible economic results, aligning every single people strategy with the corporate bottom line and maximizing resource ROI.

The Communication Rule: Translating Soft Concepts to Hard Dollars

The rule is simple: never discuss a program in terms of internal, subjective benefits. Instead, discuss the resulting external financial benefits.

- **Avoid:** Discussing a new program in terms of improving "employee satisfaction" or "morale."

- **Instead:** Talk about what satisfaction delivers for the P&L: reduced regrettable turnover, increased Time-to-Productivity (TTTP), or lower safety incidents (which translates directly to lower workers' compensation insurance premiums).

Blueprint for Financial Credibility: The Case Studies

The two case studies in this chapter illustrate the essential discipline of translating HR needs into financial terms.

The first case study, Translating Wellness to Risk Reduction (Logistics), demonstrates the power of the Finance Filter in action. The purpose of this case study is to provide a clear, step-by-step example of how to transform a commonly perceived "soft" HR program (wellness) into a direct Risk Mitigation strategy. You should use this outcome as a template to transform any internal HR benefit into an external, quantifiable cost or risk solution that secures immediate executive approval.

The second case study, "Due Diligence and the Investor Mindset (Finance)," focuses on adopting the perspective of the CEO and CFO, specifically the Investor/Owner Mindset. Its purpose is to demonstrate how HR can successfully transition a proposal from being a "cost request" to a necessary act of Due Diligence required to maintain market competitiveness. Use this example to anchor your proposals in external market data, demonstrating that your initiative is a necessary investment to protect the firm's long-term competitive value.

Case Study: Translating Wellness to Risk Reduction (Logistics) The Strategic Turnaround

The Beginning (The Tactical Pitch): The HR Director at a $95 million regional logistics company pitched a new employee wellness program to the CEO, arguing it would improve "employee well-being and morale." The CEO immediately denied the $30,000 request, stating, "We fund results, not feelings." The pitch failed because it used the wrong lexicon.

Action Taken (Strategic Resolution): The HR Director reframed the proposal entirely using the Finance Filter, with a focus on Risk Mitigation.

- **Quantified Risk:** She collected data showing the company's annual on-the-job injury rate was 15% higher than the industry average for similar logistics firms.

- **Translated Risk to Cost:** She produced a report demonstrating that this elevated injury rate directly led to $100,000 in higher workers' compensation premiums annually and an estimated $50,000 in lost productivity due to absenteeism and injury investigations. Total recurring risk: $150,000 per year.

- **Framed Proposal as Mitigation:** She returned to the CEO and presented the wellness program not as a benefit, but as a risk mitigation strategy designed to cut those recurring costs by improving driver physical health, focus, and reducing fatigue-related incidents.

Actual Outcome: The CEO approved the $30,000 program immediately because the pitch was reframed: "Invest $30,000 now to mitigate a $150,000 recurring annual risk." The HR function was immediately recognized for its role in managing enterprise risk and protecting the profit and loss (P&L) statement.

Formula in Action – Calculating Return on Investment (ROI)

ROI is the most powerful metric for justifying any financial request. It translates the cost of your HR initiative (the investment) into the financial benefit (the return) it generates for the business.[1]

ROI = Financial Benefit-Cost of Investment divided by Cost of Investment×100

Example (Using Wellness Case Study):

- **Financial Benefit (Annual Gain):** $150,000 in avoided recurring costs (insurance and lost productivity).

- **Cost of Investment (Program Cost):** $30,000.

Calculation: ROI = (150,000 − 30,000) ÷ 30,000 × 100 = 400%

Explanation: A 400% ROI proves to the executive team that your HR initiative is not a cost, but a highly profitable investment. The calculation shifts the discussion from *whether* to fund the program to *how quickly* to implement it.

5.2 The Investor/Owner Mindset

Executives, especially the CEO and CFO, fundamentally approach their organization as a large, managed asset portfolio. They view all resources: cash, equipment, and crucially, talent, as capital to be strategically deployed for maximum return and valuation growth. To gain their enduring trust, HR must appeal to this investor mindset. This means framing talent not merely as a fixed operational cost, but as a proprietary capital asset that must be invested in, developed, and protected against loss (risk). By using external market data, HR frames its talent strategy as an exercise in due diligence; the necessary research and investment required to maintain the company's competitive edge and future market valuation. The underlying question for every proposal must be: "Is this investment increasing the long-term, proprietary value of our human capital assets?"

What It Is: Framing people-related proposals as investments in a proprietary asset (human capital) that must be protected and grown to increase company value and maintain a competitive moat.

Why It's Important for the Business: It shifts the executive conversation from a tactical discussion about discretionary overhead spending (HR's cost) to a strategic debate about protecting and growing the company's future competitive advantage (talent's value).

Actionable Steps: Due Diligence and Value Creation

- **Talent Strategy as Due Diligence:** Always anchor talent needs in external market data. Demonstrate how competitors are securing the talent necessary for the company's future product roadmap. For example, if competitors are aggressively recruiting engineers with specific AI skills, HR's proposal to fund an AI upskilling program is no longer an "HR request"; it is a necessary market response driven by due diligence, removing the emotion from the debate.

- **Frame Proposals Around Value:** Every proposal should answer these three financial questions from the investor's perspective:

    o **Investment:** Is this increasing the proprietary value of our human capital asset (e.g., skill development that leads directly to new patents or product features)?

    o **Protection:** Is this mitigating a threat to the asset's value (e.g., retaining key personnel who hold unique proprietary knowledge that cannot be easily replaced)?

    o **Market Position:** Is this a necessary investment to catch up to or surpass the market's talent capability?

Case Study: Due Diligence and the Investor Mindset (Manufacturing SMB) The Production Moat

I. Context: The Challenge of the Critical Knowledge Asset

A. Organization Profile

The company Manufacturing is a family-owned, specialized metal fabrication company with 85 employees. It generates $25 million in annual revenue. The company's competitive advantage isn't volume, but its proprietary, highly efficient five-axis CNC machining processes, which have been refined over 20 years. These processes allows the company to produce complex aerospace components with significantly less waste and faster turnaround than larger competitors.

B. The SMB Talent Crisis

Their talent risk was concentrated in its small, highly specialized team. Specifically, three master machinists (who had developed the proprietary processes) and one veteran Process Engineer (who held all the undocumented workflow knowledge) were all nearing retirement within five years.

The CEO and the CFO viewed the three-person HR team as an administrative function focused on payroll and compliance. When HR proposed a $50,000 budget for a "Knowledge Transfer and Apprenticeship Program," the CFO immediately rejected it: "We can't afford that overhead. Continue recruiting until you find suitable replacements. We need to save cash."

HR was failing to speak the language of the Investor/Owner Mindset, framing the proposal as a cost instead of a critical investment in the firm's core intellectual property.

II. The Strategic Solution: Talent Strategy as Due Diligence

A. The Risk-Adjusted Proposal

The HR team re-framed the entire discussion around asset valuation and operational risk mitigation. The new proposal was titled: "Protecting Our Proprietary Manufacturing Moat: A Due Diligence Requirement."

B. Due Diligence: Quantifying the Financial Risk

HR performed due diligence by calculating the financial impact of losing the critical knowledge assets:

1. **Cost of Loss (Protection Risk):** HR calculated that losing the Master Machinists would immediately halt production on two key aerospace contracts for an estimated 6-9 months, leading to $3 million in liquidated damages and lost revenue.

2. **Market Scarcity (Market Position):** HR analyzed external job market data (local trade schools, competitor listings). They found that the cost and time (2+ years) to externally hire and integrate a single machinist with *similar* capabilities exceeded the apprenticeship program's cost by 300%.

This data showed the CFO that relying on external hiring was not a cash-saving measure; it was a catastrophic financial gamble.

III. Execution: Answering the Three Financial Questions

The revised proposal was presented as an investment necessity to the CEO and CFO:

1. Investment: Is this increasing the proprietary value of our human capital asset?

- **The Investment:** The $50,000 program was to be split between stipends for the four retiring experts to document their processes and stipends for four new internal apprentices.

- **Value Creation:** The program's core goal was not just replacing people but codifying the undocumented knowledge. HR argued that by turning tacit knowledge into documented, teachable IP, the company was increasing the proprietary, defensible value of its processes. The apprentices would learn the unique "The Company Way," creating a truly proprietary, highly efficient Human Capital Asset that could not be easily copied.

- **Outcome:** The investment was positioned as building a "production moat" (a sustainable competitive advantage), ensuring that the company's unique low-waste advantage remained an internal asset, increasing the firm's overall valuation in the eyes of future investors or buyers.

2. Protection: Is this mitigating a threat to the assets' value?

- **The Threat:** The immediate threat was the loss of key personnel and the undocumented process knowledge they held.

- **Protection Strategy:** The program was framed as "Key-Person Insurance." By accelerating the transfer of critical knowledge, The company was mitigating the massive $3 million risk of a production shutdown. HR ensured the CFO understood this was a necessary risk management expense, not an optional training cost. Furthermore, providing a structured exit for the veterans and a clear career path for younger workers protected the morale and engagement of the entire small workforce.

3. Market Position: Is this a necessary investment to catch up to or surpass the market's talent capability?

- **The Proposition:** The company could not afford to compete with large firms on salary for top external talent. The apprenticeship program allowed the company to "build vs. buy" at a significantly lower cost and with higher quality.

- **Market Advantage:** HR demonstrated that by formalizing the apprenticeship, the company would become the only local SMB actively creating this specific, high-demand skill set. This enhanced reputation made the company a far more attractive, strategic choice for young talent leaving trade schools, effectively giving them a competitive advantage in the local talent market.

IV. **Conclusion**: The Strategic Transformation

The HR team's use of external market data and the quantification of financial risk successfully spoke to the CEO and CFO's Investor/Owner mindset. They approved the $50,000 investment.

Within one year, the program successfully documented the four core proprietary processes and had the apprentices confidently managing 50% of the workload. This transformation proved that, even for an SMB with a tight cash flow, talent is not an overhead cost but a proprietary asset that requires deliberate, data-driven investment to ensure the company's long-term survival and maintain a competitive moat. The HR function had successfully transitioned from an administrative unit to a strategic driver of asset protection and value creation.

5.3 Conciseness is Currency

Discussion: Executive time is the most expensive and limited resource in the organization. Therefore, conciseness is currency: it is the measure of respect you pay to the leadership team. Long, dense reports or detailed, 50-slide presentations are not viewed as thorough; they are viewed as roadblocks and a failure of the presenter to filter information. Strategic HR must master the art of boiling down a complex people problem, such as high regrettable turnover, to its essential financial components and its solution. This requires disciplined formatting, ensuring that the financial implications are always front-loaded and immediately accessible.

What It Is: Mastering the ability to deliver complex analytical information in highly condensed formats, such as the One-Page Proposal or the Three-Slide Deck, which respects executive attention limits.

Why It's Important for the Business: It respects the executive team's limited time and ensures the key financial data necessary for decision-making is immediately accessible, accelerating strategic approval processes from weeks to minutes.

The One-Page Proposal

This document is ideal for proposals that require an initial budgetary review. It must contain four concise, numbered sections, with the financial impact emphasized upfront:

- **The Problem (The Pain Point):** Define the problem in executive terms (e.g., "Loss of key talent is delaying Q3 product roadmap completion.").

- **The Data (The Proof):** State the quantifiable evidence using strategic metrics (e.g., "Regrettable turnover in the R&D department is 25%,15% above the industry benchmark.").

- **The Solution (The Action):** The specific, focused, and concise initiative (e.g., "Implement a $50,000 targeted retention bonus structure and mentorship program for R&D.").

- **The ROI (The Payoff):** The projected financial benefit, using the Finance Filter (e.g., "This investment protects against a $400,000 penalty from delayed Q3 launch and reduces projected turnover to 10%.")

Three-Slide Deck

This framework is ideal for brief, verbal reviews and updates, often delivered in 5 minutes or less:

- **Slide 1: The Problem & The Cost:** Clearly state the operational or financial pain point, supported by the quantifiable metric. *Example:* "High R&D Turnover (25%) is costing us an estimated $12,000 per week in lost project velocity."

- **Slide 2: The Solution & The Investment Required:** Detail the specific action and the precise budget/resources needed. *Example:* "We need $50,000 for the retention bonus program, implemented immediately."

- **Slide 3: The Projected Return & Next Steps:** State the financial payoff and clearly define what action you need the executive to approve today. *Example:* "This investment yields 8X ROI. We need immediate approval of the $50,000 transfer to the retention fund by 5 PM today."

Chapter 5 Checklist: Speaking the Language of the C-Suite

Action	Outcome
Action 1: Practice converting three current HR programs (e.g., leadership training, new compensation plan) into	Ensures every proposal is framed as a financial decision.

Action	Outcome
a mandatory Cost, Revenue, and Risk statement.	
Action 2: Draft a One-Page Proposal for your next major initiative, ensuring the first paragraph focuses only on the quantifiable financial impact (The Pain Point).	Creates a clear, concise, and immediately impactful document for executive review.
Action 3: Find external market data showing a competitor's recent talent investment to frame your proposal as due diligence or a necessary market response.	Adds necessary external validation to your proposal (appeals to the investor mindset).

Key Takeaways

- **Language is Power:** Always translate internal HR concepts (e.g., morale) into the executive lexicon of Cost, Revenue, and Risk via the Finance Filter.

- **Talent as Capital:** Adopt the Investor/Owner Mindset, framing people-related spending as an investment in a proprietary, value-generating asset that must be protected and grown.

- **Conciseness is Respect:** Master the One-Page Proposal and Three-Slide Deck to ensure the financial argument is front-loaded and immediately consumable by the executive team.

- **Front-Load the Payoff:** Never lead with the problem; always lead with the cost and risk of *not* solving the problem.

Reflection

Use these questions to spark discussion with your leadership team.

- What is the single biggest financial risk currently posed by a "people problem" (e.g., skill deficit, leadership vacancy) in the organization?

- If we framed our current leadership development program as a capital investment, what is the current ROI we can demonstrate to the CFO?

- In our next executive meeting, how can we ensure the first 60 seconds of our presentation focus solely on the financial consequences of the problem?
- What external talent market data can we use to prove to the CEO that our upcoming talent initiative is an act of competitive due diligence?

Chapter 6: Gaining Executive Buy-In (The Proof-of-Concept Strategy)

Summary:

Chapter 6 outlines the Proof-of-Concept (PoC) strategy, the most effective way for HR to earn executive buy-in. A PoC is a small, contained, high-visibility pilot project designed to target the executive's most pressing pain point and generate rapid, quantifiable, positive financial results. This mitigates risk, transforms skepticism into enthusiasm, and enables the HR leader to transition to a Trusted Advisor role.

Step-by-Step Framework

The executive suite operates under a high-stakes, result-oriented culture where time is currency, and every expenditure is viewed through the lens of risk. While Chapter 5 provided the necessary lexicon for strategic communication, Chapter 6 provides the methodology for securing and sustaining executive support. Executives are inherently risk-averse to new expenditures, especially in areas they perceive as "soft" or difficult to measure (such as talent programs or leadership training). The most effective way to dismantle this financial resistance and earn credibility is the Proof-of-Concept (PoC) strategy. A PoC is not a full program launch; it is a small, contained, high-visibility pilot project designed to generate rapid, quantifiable, and positive financial results within a short, defined period (usually 90 days). It effectively mitigates executive risk by requesting a small, measured investment to definitively prove the large-scale ROI (Return on Investment), thereby transforming executive skepticism into enthusiastic buy-in for a company-wide rollout.

Proof of Concept Lifecycle

The strategic success of a Proof-of-Concept hinges on accurately identifying and targeting an acute pain point, a specific business problem that the CEO or President is currently complaining about, as it directly impacts revenue, margins, or core operations. This is likely the most expensive and most visible issue within the organization. Examples might include chronically high turnover in a single, revenue-generating team (like Sales Development) or a specific, measurable rate of consistent product failure in one production unit. By focusing your initial, low-risk strategic effort on an area that is already a source of executive frustration and high financial drag, you ensure two key benefits: maximum executive attention and the certainty that a successful outcome will be immediately recognized as valuable to the entire organization. This strategic choice positions HR as a problem-solver from day one.

What It Is: Identifying a high-visibility, small, and contained group (the pilot) to test a focused, low-cost strategic solution. The group should be chosen not for convenience, but for its high impact on the P&L and the speed with which its results can be measured.

Why It's Important for the Business: It generates quick wins and builds immediate credibility. By solving a visible, costly problem that other departments have failed to fix, HR demonstrates its functional capability to manage critical business outcomes, not just administer policies.

Actionable Steps (Month 2 Action)

- **Select the Target:** The pilot must be small enough that the intervention can be managed easily and the results measured quickly (within 90 days), yet visible enough that its success cannot be ignored. A perfect target is often the Sales Development Representative (SDR) team, a highly measurable and high-turnover group directly linked to the revenue pipeline.

- **Design Intervention:** Design a focused, 90-day intervention specifically for that pilot team. If the pain point is turnover, the intervention might be enhanced retention and onboarding focused specifically on improving manager coaching skills and implementing a weekly accountability check-in.

- **Rule:** The PoC must be high-impact, low-cost, and clearly measurable (using metrics established in Chapter 3) to maximize the financial impact relative to the investment. Asking for only $5,000 to solve a $100,000 problem minimizes executive risk.

Pilot Selection Criteria

Pilot Selection Criteria	
Visibility	☐
Cost	☐
Time to Result	☐
Measurability	☐

The Case Studies

The two case studies in this chapter are designed to demonstrate the indispensable power of the Proof-of-Concept (PoC) strategy.

Case Study 1: PoC to Strategic Mandate (Engineering Firm)

The Challenge: Mitigating Project Manager Turnover

A 120-employee civil engineering firm specializing in public infrastructure was facing a critical talent retention issue. Losing a Project Manager (PM) was costly; the firm's internal analysis estimated the total replacement cost (including recruiting, training, and lost billable hours) at $40,000 per manager.

The acute pain point was the high PM turnover rate of 20%, resulting in the loss of approximately four PMs annually. This is translated to an annualized, unbudgeted Cost of Replacement of $160,000.

The 90-Day Proof-of-Concept (PoC)

The HR Leader requested a minimal budget of $10,000 for a 90-day, targeted intervention called the "PM Support Loop," applied to a pilot group of 5 PMs.

The Intervention:

- **Resource Allocation Training:** Focused on empowering PMs with better self-management and delegation tools.

- **Senior Mentorship:** Paired the pilot group with an experienced senior engineer to provide confidential technical mentorship and reduce burnout.

The Data Showcase: Translating Retention into Cost Avoidance

After 90 days, the results were presented to the executive suite, with a focus exclusively on the financial impact.

Metric	Before PoC (Baseline - Company Avg.)	After PoC (90-Day Pilot Group)	Financial Impact (Annualized)
PM Turnover Rate	20%	5% (Annualized Rate)	Projected $120,000 in Cost Avoidance
Employee Net Promoter Score (eNPS)*	-10	+35	Improved morale reduces secondary turnover risk.

*Employee Net Promoter Score (eNPS) is a metric that measures employee satisfaction and engagement by asking them to rate on a scale of 0-10 how likely they are to recommend their company as a place to work. The score is calculated by subtracting the percentage of detractors (those who score 0-6) from the percentage of promoters (those who score 9-10), providing a single score that ranges from -100 to +100.

The Financial Translation:

The 15% reduction in the annualized turnover rate (20% to 5%$) meant the firm avoided the need to replace 3 Project Managers over the next year (based on the 20-person PM team size).

3 PMs Avoided X $40,000 Cost per Replacement = $120,000 Annual Cost Avoidance.

Outcome: Securing Strategic Mandate

This case study demonstrates how to address a critical pain point (losing expensive project managers) and implement a targeted intervention to achieve substantial, quantifiable Cost Savings. The HR function successfully turned a $10,000 investment into an annualized $120,000 financial result.

This provides a complete blueprint for translating a minimal budget request into a full, company-wide strategic mandate, moving from a $10,000 investment to a $50,000 rollout (justified by the $120,000 saving). This outcome serves as a model to show how 90 days of focused effort can immediately secure an HR leader's Trusted Advisor status.

PoC Financial Payoff

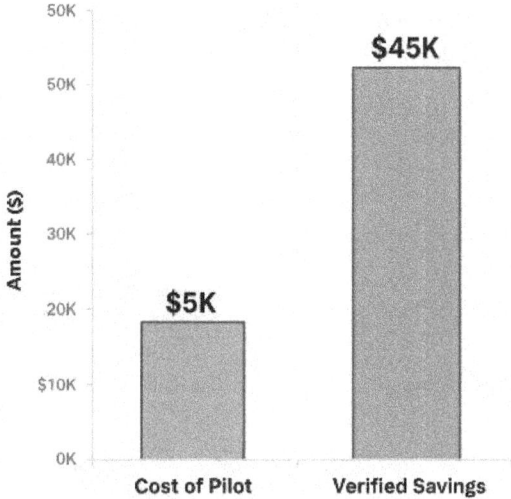

6.2 The Data Showcase: Quantitative Results

The actual intervention of the PoC is secondary; the primary goal is the Data Showcase. Once the 90-day pilot is complete, the HR function must immediately present the results using a simple before-and-after analysis. This presentation must translate the improvement directly into the financial language of cost reduction and revenue acceleration. The focus should not be on internal metrics, such as "training satisfaction scores," but on how much money the program generated or saved.

What It Is: Presenting the PoC results using simple quantitative metrics (e.g., turnover rate, TTTP) and translating the improvement directly into financial consequences that appear on the executive scorecard.

Why It's Important for the Business: It provides the executive suite with empirical evidence that the HR strategy delivers a positive financial ROI. This quantitative validation is the non-negotiable step necessary to justify the company-wide rollout of the initiative and secure the larger budget required.

Metric	Before PoC (Baseline)	After PoC (90 Days)	Financial Impact (Annualized)
SDR Turnover Rate	45%	30%	Projected $120,000 saved in replacement costs annually.
Time-to-Productivity (SDR)	12 weeks	9 weeks	25% faster revenue contribution 3 weeks of accelerated sales revenue per hire).

Proven Results – PoC on Revenue Acceleration

The second callout, Proven Result, is an additional example that shows the PoC strategy applied to Revenue Acceleration. Its purpose is to broaden your toolkit by demonstrating a measured increase in sales output, proving that HR interventions not only reduce costs but can also directly increase revenue.

A 150-person B2B sales firm ran a 90-day Proof-of-Concept on its lowest-performing sales team (10 people). The $4,000 PoC investment was used for focused management training on goal-setting and weekly 1:1 coaching.

The result was a measurable increase in new sales activity (prospecting calls and booked meetings). In the 90 days, the pilot group's average qualified lead generation increased by 25% compared to the baseline. This 25% increase was then presented to the CEO as a direct $75,000 acceleration of pipeline revenue, immediately justifying a $50,000 rollout of the training program to the entire sales management team.

You should use both outcomes to build a library of proven financial results that justify future strategic investments.

6.3 The Trusted Advisor Shift

Narrative Discussion: Consistent, data-driven delivery of positive financial results, like the successful PoC, is the only way to shift the executive perception of the HR leader from an administrative compliance officer (the "policy police") to a Trusted Advisor. This advisory status is earned through demonstrated Reliability (following through on promises and delivering quantifiable outcomes) and absolute Confidentiality (managing sensitive information and financial details with professional discretion). The ultimate sign of this strategic shift is when leaders from other functions, the VP of Operations, the Head of Engineering, or the CFO, begin actively seeking HR's advice on non-HR-related operational challenges, viewing HR as an invaluable resource for problem-solving, risk mitigation, and overall strategy formulation.

What It Is: A sustained change in executive perception where the HR leader is sought out for advice on organizational, operational, and strategic challenges that extend beyond traditional HR boundaries.

Why It's Important for the Business: It ensures the people strategy is integrated into all major corporate decisions, from acquisitions to market entry, mitigating talent risks proactively and ensuring human capital considerations are factored into every strategic move, thereby maximizing the probability of success.

6.4 The Role of the HR Leader: Beyond People Management

Narrative Discussion: To successfully achieve and maintain the Trusted Advisor status, the HR leader must demonstrate business acumen, not simply expertise in people management. The expertise must transcend the HR handbook. This requires continuous professional development that targets core business competencies, validating the HR leader as a peer to the CFO and VP of Operations.

Required Competencies for Peer Status

- **Financial Literacy:** The leader must be financially literate enough to read and interpret the company's P&L statement and Balance Sheet. Understanding the drivers of profit and loss (e.g., Gross Margin, Cost of Goods Sold) allows the HR leader to identify where people problems are directly damaging the firm's finances.

- **Operational Context:** The leader must possess deep operational context, understanding how the company genuinely creates value: how products are made, how services are delivered, and where critical bottlenecks occur in the value chain. This allows HR to propose interventions that solve the operational problem, not just the people symptoms.

- **Courage to Say No:** The leader must possess the courage to strategically push back on frivolous (non-ROI-generating) requests from executives. This discipline ensures that limited budget and HR capacity are directed only toward high-priority, high-impact initiatives, maintaining the function's strategic focus and financial credibility.

Case Study: PoC to Strategic Mandate (Engineering Firm) The Strategic Turnaround

Issue: A $150 million engineering firm was losing its most experienced project managers (PMs) to voluntary turnover (35% annualized), costing the firm an estimated $450,000 in replacement costs and project delays. The CEO viewed the problem as "salary demands."

Action Taken (The PoC and Data Showcase): The HR Director secured a $10,000 budget for a 90-day PoC on the smallest, highest-cost project management team. The intervention was simple: mandatory skip-level meetings for PMs (to increase visibility and address issues without a manager filter) and a structured career mapping program.

- **Baseline:** Before the PoC, the team's regrettable turnover rate was 40%.

- **Intervention & Showcase:** After 90 days, the PoC team's turnover rate dropped to 10% annualized. The Director presented the data to the executive committee, framing the $10,000 investment against the $180,000 in replacement costs saved for that one team.

Outcome: The CEO immediately approved a $120,000 budget to roll out the career mapping and skip-level meeting structure across the entire firm, officially recognizing the HR strategy as the solution to their talent hemorrhaging. This earned the HR Director the Trusted Advisor status, leading to her being consulted on a subsequent acquisition strategy to assess the target firm's organizational risk.

Chapter 6 Checklist: Gaining Executive Buy-In

Action	Outcome
Action 1: Secure approval and a small budget for a Proof-of-Concept (PoC) to address the CEO's primary pain point.	A focused, low-risk project with high visibility and potential for high financial return.
Action 2: Complete the PoC and prepare a Before-and-After Data Showcase, focusing exclusively on the financial impact using Cost, Revenue, and Risk language.	Demonstrated ROI and earned initial executive confidence, justifying broader investment.
Action 3: Study the company's recent quarterly or annual financial statements (P&L and Balance Sheet) to improve your Financial Literacy.	The foundational skill for speaking the C-Suite language as a peer.

Key Takeaways

- **PoC is Risk Mitigation:** Use the Proof-of-Concept (PoC) strategy—a low-cost, high-impact pilot—to mitigate executive spending risk and generate rapid, measurable financial wins.

- **Target Acute Pain:** Focus the PoC on the specific, visible, and costly problem the executive team is currently complaining about for maximum attention and credit.

- **The Data Showcase:** The success of the PoC lies in the before-and-after data presentation, translating improvement directly into saved costs and accelerated revenue.

- **Trusted Advisor Status:** Earn peer status by demonstrating Reliability and Confidentiality, and by possessing the Financial Literacy and Operational Context to solve problems beyond traditional HR boundaries.

Reflection

Use these questions to spark discussion with your leadership team.

- What is the single most visible, costly operational problem currently causing executive frustration that we can address with a 90-day PoC?

- If we were to run a PoC, how would we ensure the data collected translates directly into dollars saved or revenue accelerated?

- Which non-HR executive (e.g., CFO, COO) is currently facing a bottleneck that our people strategy could solve, and how can we use our PoC to earn their trust?

- Do we, as a leadership team, possess enough operational context to accurately pinpoint the true drivers of profit and loss in the business?

Chapter 7: Managing the Skepticism and the "Soft Stuff" Critique

Summary

The Strategic HR function must proactively neutralize the inevitable "soft stuff" critique by anticipating executive skepticism and providing data-driven counter-arguments. This chapter provides the tools to prove that culture and talent systems are not subjective feel-good measures, but are, in fact, the essential operating system of results that can be directly linked to hard financial outcomes and institutionalized on the Executive Scorecard.

Step-by-Step Framework.

Even after successfully demonstrating success with a Proof-of-Concept (PoC) (Chapter 6), the Strategic HR function will inevitably face resistance rooted in the "soft stuff" critique. This is the persistent executive challenge that dismisses talent initiatives (such as leadership training, engagement programs, or culture design) as non-essential, "touchy-feely" activities lacking a measurable financial return. Overcoming this skepticism permanently requires the HR leader to be prepared with data-driven counterarguments that prove culture and talent systems are not merely feel-good measures but are the very operating system that drives results for the entire business. This chapter provides the analytical and communication tools to proactively anticipate and neutralize these objections, permanently embedding HR's role in the organization's formal accountability structure.

7.1 Anticipating Objections: Neutralizing Resistance with Data

Discussion: A hallmark of the Trusted Advisor (Chapter 6) is the ability to anticipate executive resistance before it is even voiced.

Executive objections often stem from a fundamental misunderstanding: they view HR's work as disconnected from the operational profit engine of the business. The key is to reframe their concerns, showing that your strategic work is focused on fixing underlying systemic and structural problems that generate recurring, quantifiable costs. By having prepared, quantitative rebuttals ready, you prevent the discussion from descending into a subjective debate about "feelings" and immediately pivoted back to measurable financial impact and risk mitigation.

What It Is: Proactively developing data-driven counter-arguments to common executive dismissals regarding talent initiatives, ensuring the conversation remains focused on business results. This requires rehearsing the rebuttal until it becomes an immediate, automatic strategic response.

Why It's Important for the Business: It ensures strategic initiatives are not derailed by old, generalized mindsets, protecting the momentum and investment made in the transformation. Derailed initiatives lead to wasted budget and lost credibility.

Common Objections and Strategic Counter-Arguments

Executive Objection	Strategic Counter-Argument (Reframed to Cost/Risk)	Detailed Explanation
"Why do we need a new process? Just hire better people."	Counter-Argument: "Hiring better people is the outcome of a strategic HR system, not the solution itself. A regrettable turnover rate is not just a hiring problem; it's a structural issue (e.g., inadequate manager training, lack of career development opportunities). Our strategic initiatives fix the underlying system that allows poor performance	The core flaw in the objection is the belief that talent retention is purely a recruitment issue. You must prove it's a systemic problem solved by better management systems, which HR is responsible for designing and measuring.

Executive Objection	Strategic Counter-Argument (Reframed to Cost/Risk)	Detailed Explanation
	and high turnover to persist, protecting the investment made in hiring top talent."	
"Culture is touchy-feely. We focus on results and P&L."	Counter-Argument: "Culture is the operating system of results. Toxic cultural behaviors (e.g., lack of communication, internal conflict) are costing us in safety incidents, insurance claims, and project rework each year, or they're accelerating project failure. We're using data to manage the soft stuff the way Operations manages hard assets, because behavior drives measurable cost and risk."	Culture is not about morale; it's about predictable behavior. If behaviors are toxic, they introduce financial risk (fines, lawsuits, premium hikes, and project delays). Strategic HR uses data to manage these behaviors.

COMMON MISTAKE – Confusing Activity with Health

A frequent executive mistake is equating high activity with structural health. For instance, an executive might point to an overloaded HR team and say, "They're too busy to take on a strategic project." The strategic response must clarify that high activity is often a symptom of poor structure. If HR is constantly busy solving the same recurring employee conflicts (high activity), it means the underlying management system is broken (poor health). The strategic intervention focuses on fixing the system, the structural cause, to reduce the activity over time.

Blueprint for Silencing Skepticism: The Case Study

The single case study in this chapter, Linking Engagement to COGS (Manufacturing), is designed to provide the definitive, measurable proof required to silence the "soft stuff" critique.

Its purpose is to teach you how to execute a data correlation analysis that links a traditionally "soft" cultural element (manager communication/engagement scores) directly to a hard financial metric (Cost of Goods Sold/Defect Rate). By demonstrating that a low communication score leads to measurable, costly defects, you transform the HR initiative from a "nice-to-have" training program into a mandatory, cost-saving operational fix. You should use the outcome as a universal model for analyzing your own organizational data: identify the cultural metric your executive dismisses and demonstrate its direct correlation to a financial pain point that the executive cares about (Cost, Revenue, or Risk).

7.2 Linking Culture to Profit: The Data Correlation

Cultural ROI Index
Mapping Engagement to Financial Performance

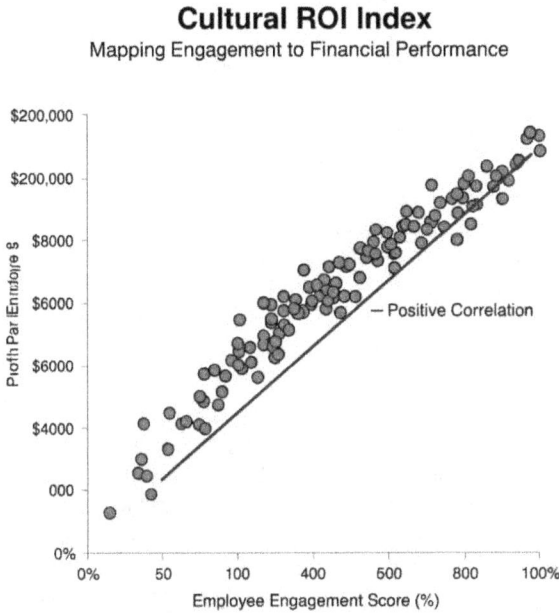

Discussion: To permanently silence the "soft stuff" critique, you must move beyond defensive arguments and proactively prove that cultural elements, like trust, engagement, and inclusion, are directly correlated with hard business outputs. This requires rigorous analysis (often using data from your HRIS, internal engagement surveys, or organizational network analysis) to establish a clear, statistically significant cause-and-effect relationship. When culture is shown to reduce defects, accelerate project completion, or increase patent generation, it ceases to be "soft" and becomes an essential Profit Enabler, measurable driver of business success.

What It Is: Establishing a clear, measurable correlation between internal cultural factors (e.g., employee survey results on trust or psychological safety) and external financial or operational results (e.g., quality ratings, project speed, revenue per employee).

Why It's Important for the Business: It validates cultural design as a high-value strategic function, proving that culture is a management tool for controlling financial risk and accelerating innovation, rather than a discretionary expense.

Proving the Correlation: From Survey Data to P&L Impact

- **Engagement vs. Quality:** Do not just report the engagement score. Segment the organization by department or unit. Show how teams with the highest engagement scores (e.g., top quartile) have a lower rate of manufacturing defects or higher quality assurance ratings compared to the lowest-scoring teams. This directly links engagement to the Cost of Goods Sold (COGS) and brand reputation risk.

- **Trust vs. Speed:** Correlate team trust levels (measured via internal surveys on psychological safety and peer support) with operational outputs like project completion times or service delivery speed. High-trust teams often move faster because they waste less time on internal politics, bureaucracy, and verification checks. The resulting time savings translate directly to accelerated revenue recognition or faster time-to-market.

- **Inclusion vs. Innovation:** Demonstrate how diverse teams, backed by inclusive cultural practices (where all voices are heard and feel safe to challenge ideas), generate a higher number of approved patents or successful new product feature ideas per year. This links cultural health to the organization's capacity for Revenue Generation and Competitive Advantage, proving that diversity is an innovation catalyst.

Case Study: Linking Engagement to COGS (Manufacturing)
The Strategic Turnaround Issue:

A $100M specialty manufacturer faced recurring quality control failures, leading to high warranty costs and delayed shipments. The VP of Operations blamed equipment age, while HR believed the cause was a lack of motivation.

Action Taken (Data Correlation): The HR Director used the newly implemented HRIS to merge quarterly employee engagement survey data with the Operations team's quality assurance metrics (defect rate per unit). The analysis showed that the two production lines with the lowest in "My manager communicates effectively" scores had a higher defect rate than the two lines with the highest scores. The correlation proved that the problem was not machine failure, but communication failure leading to human error.

Outcome: The HR Director presented the data to the executive team: "We can invest in new equipment, or we can invest in manager communication training to save an estimated on annual warranty and rework costs." The training was approved immediately, linking the "soft skill" of communication directly to Cost of Goods Sold and financial savings.

7.3 Institutionalizing Strategy: The Executive Scorecard

The final and most decisive step in securing HR's strategic authority is to make the function non-negotiable by embedding its key metrics into the firm's formal accountability structure. This is achieved by advocating for the inclusion of critical HR risk metrics on the organization's overall Executive Scorecard. The Executive Scorecard is the official, top-level summary of performance metrics for which the CEO and the Board are held accountable (e.g., Quarterly Revenue, Gross Margin, Customer Acquisition Cost). By placing key talent risks (like the Succession Readiness Score) alongside financial results, you force executive attention and funding, ensuring the strategic HR function is permanently valued because its metrics directly influence the leadership team's bonus structure and accountability. If a metric is on the scorecard, it cannot be ignored during budget cuts.

What It Is: Formally integrating HR's key risk and value metrics into the top-level performance reporting used by the CEO and Board. This moves the metric from an HR report to an enterprise indicator of health and risk.

Why It's Important for the Business: It makes the entire executive team accountable for talent management outcomes, transforming talent strategy from an HR concern into an enterprise risk concern that cannot be ignored during budget cuts.

Executive Scorecard View

Connecting HR to Financial Performance

← HR Metrics →
Financial KPIS

Turnovor %

8%

Financial Impact:
$1.2M Annual Cost

Absenteeism

3.5%

Financial Impact:
$450K Lost Productiv

Quality Cost

$2.5M

Financial Impact:
15% Revenue Loss

Safety Cost

$300K

Financial Impact:
10% Insurance Reduction

Strategic HR Metrics to Include on the Executive Scorecard

Strategic HR Metric	Measures	Financial Justification to the CFO
Succession Readiness Score	Talent Risk	Quantifies the vulnerability to leadership loss. Failure to fund succession planning is a direct risk to future valuation and operations.
Cost of Regrettable Turnover (YTD)	Financial Cost	The actual, measurable dollars lost due to voluntary departures of high performers. This metric is the

Strategic HR Metric	Measures	Financial Justification to the CFO
		annual tax on poor management systems.
Skills Gap Analysis Score	Adaptability Risk	A metric showing the percentage of future required skills (from the - year roadmap) currently missing. This predicts future revenue bottlenecks and acquisition needs.

Chapter 7 Checklist: Managing Skepticism

Action	Outcome
Action 1: Inventory the top three executive objections you currently receive and draft data-driven counter-arguments, focusing on reframing the objection as a **Cost** or **Risk** issue.	Preparation to maintain authority and avoid losing strategic focus.
Action 2: Identify one cultural element (e.g., team trust score) and perform a rigorous analysis correlating it with a hard output (e.g., project completion speed or defect rate).	Generates data that proves culture is a .
Action 3: Draft a formal proposal to include the Succession Readiness Score and the Cost of Regrettable Turnover on the official Executive Scorecard.	Embeds HR risk and financial metrics into the firm's top-level accountability structure.

Key Takeaways

- **Culture is the Operating System:** Counter the "soft stuff" critique by proving that culture is the measurable operating system of results, not morale.

- **Proactive Rebuttal:** Anticipate executive skepticism and have quantitative rebuttals ready to immediately pivot the conversation back to cost and risk.

- **Prove the Correlation:** Use rigorous data analysis to establish a direct link between internal talent metrics (e.g., engagement, trust) and external financial metrics (e.g., quality, speed, COGS).

- **Institutionalize Accountability:** Achieve permanence by embedding key risk metrics, such as the Succession Readiness Score, on the Executive Scorecard, making talent management an enterprise accountability.

Proactive Rebuttal Framework

Adressing Executive Objections with Data & Finance

Objection	Data Response	Financial Reframe
HR is a cost center.	Show unit cost reduction from correlate	Cost optimization: $500K saved annualy
Culture initiatives are 'soft'	High-engagement teams correlate with +20%	Revenue increase: $1.2M from output boost
Training is too expensive	Upskilled employees fill 70% of senior roles internally	Avoided hiring costs: $300K/year, Time-to-Productivity

Reflection

Use these questions to spark discussion with your leadership team.

- What is the current cultural behavior (e.g., conflict avoidance, micromanagement) that is most measurably delaying our project timelines or increasing our operational costs?

- If we were to measure the correlation between manager communication scores and the cost of defects, what is the conservative annual savings we could promise the CEO?

- Which key talent metric are we currently tracking that has the highest potential to be accepted onto the formal Executive Scorecard?

- What is the -to- scale rating of our leadership team's belief that "soft initiatives" (like training) lead directly to hard financial results?

Chapter 8: Understanding the Turf War Dynamics

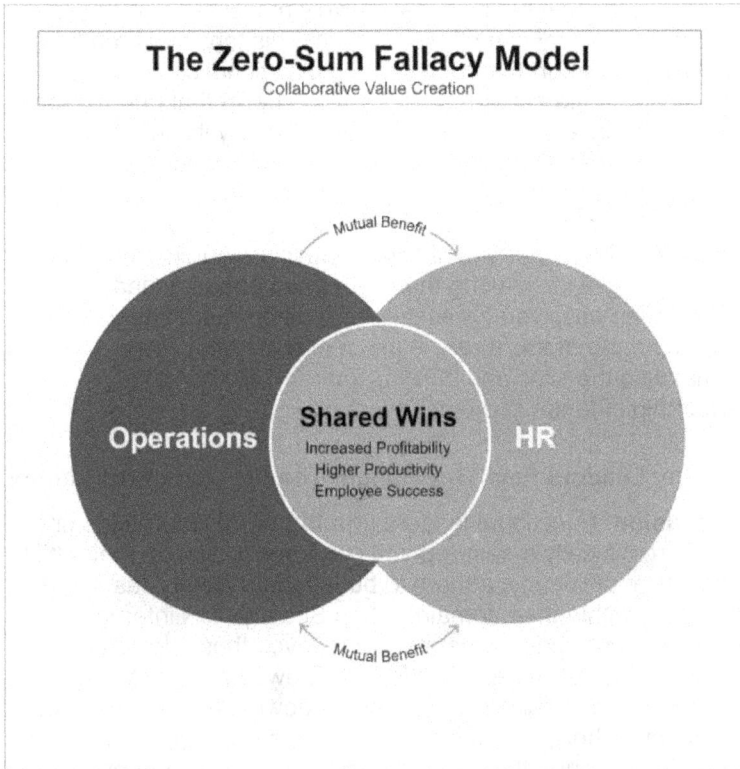

The Zero-Sum Fallacy Model

Collaborative Value Creation

Mutual Benefit

Operations

Shared Wins
Increased Profitability
Higher Productivity
Employee Success

HR

Mutual Benefit

Summary

The shift to Strategic HR often sparks a turf war with peer executives (CFO, VP of Ops) who perceive HR's new authority as a threat to their autonomy and control over departmental budgets and processes. Understanding that this friction stems from the zero-sum fallacy allows the HR leader to neutralize resistance by acting as the ultimate Integrator, demonstrating how HR's success creates measurable benefits for every other function.

Step-by-Step Framework

The moment the HR function successfully transitions from being a necessary compliance center (a role executives rarely notice or fear) to a strategic function that actively measures and drives business value, friction often emerges. This tension is rarely personal; it is a turf war rooted in organizational structure, specifically in the zero-sum fallacy —the belief that one person's gain in influence must mean another's loss. By its very nature, Strategic HR must establish common systems and standards for key departmental decisions (e.g., standardizing hiring processes, performance management, and compensation structures). This imposition challenges the historical, absolute autonomy of functional leaders, making them feel threatened and leading to active, often passive-aggressive, resistance. Understanding the precise nature of this threat is the crucial first step toward dismantling the silos and building shared, collaborative ownership of talent strategy.

8.1 Why Leaders Feel Threatened: The Erosion of Autonomy

Discussion: Functional leaders (like the VP of Operations or CTO) are typically measured and rewarded based on their ability to maintain efficiency, adhere to budget, and ensure fast execution within their domain. When Strategic HR intervenes to implement enterprise-wide standards, even those designed for the firm's long-term benefit, it is often viewed as introducing administrative bureaucracy that slows down the leader's direct control over their operational metrics. This perceived threat crystallizes around three key, sacred areas of departmental control:

- **Budget Control (The Money Threat):** HR's proposals, such as standardizing compensation bands across the firm based on market data, or mandating and funding company-wide training initiatives, often impose rules or non-negotiable costs on departmental budgets. The functional leader loses their sole discretion over how to spend their "people money" and feels their agility in rewarding or hiring is being limited by an outside party.

- **Hiring Autonomy (The Authority Threat):** Strategic workforce planning and the implementation of standardized recruiting processes (like the Candidate Interview Loop) directly challenge the deeply held belief that a department manager can hire whoever they want, whenever they want, based solely on personal preference or instinct. This is viewed by the peer executive as HR interfering with their fundamental right to build their team according to their own judgment, regardless of the quality-of-hire data.

- **Data Ownership (The Competence Threat):** This is the most sensitive area. When HR uses objective, enterprise-wide data (e.g., regrettable turnover rates, Time-to-Productivity) to critique an operational weakness within a peer's domain (e.g., high turnover in a specific sales territory), the functional leader may perceive this as a public attack on their competence and a direct threat to their internal authority and established reporting structure. HR is seen as "policing" their failures with data.

What It Is: The systemic friction that arises when HR's strategic authority (standardizing systems for enterprise benefit) challenges a functional leader's autonomy (managing their department without external constraints).

Why It's Important for the Business: This dynamic, if left unchecked, leads to crippling **functional silos,** where departments actively work against HR initiatives, sabotaging enterprise-wide strategic goals such as standardization and cost reduction.

8.2 Identifying the Primary Threats: Who Fears What

Shared Savings Opportunity

Financial Benefits of HR & Operations Collaboration

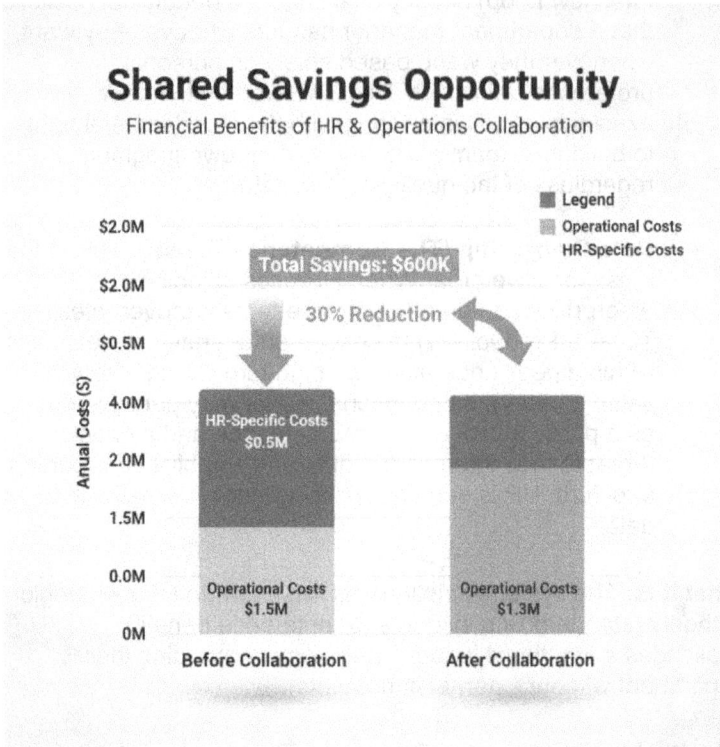

Discussion: Resistance from peer functions is highly predictable because it centers directly on the core responsibility of the executive being challenged by HR's new metrics or systems. The Strategic HR leader must use this understanding to anticipate the core of the disagreement and negotiate based on mutual business benefit, rather than engaging in a departmental contest for power.

Peer Function	The Perceived Threat	The Turf War Is Over...
Finance (CFO)	The Metrics Threat: HR's new metrics (e.g., Cost of Regrettable Turnover)	The definitive measure of organizational performance and the

Peer Function	The Perceived Threat	The Turf War Is Over...
	compete with traditional financial metrics for space on the executive scorecard and resource allocation.	authority to allocate capital and budgetary resources.

Common Mistake – The Cost Center Label

The primary source of the turf war with the CFO is the failure to measure Human Capital ROI (HC-ROI). A tactical HR budget is merely a list of costs (salaries, benefits, training). The CFO will constantly treat this as a Cost Center to be cut. Strategic HR must counter this by consistently reporting HC-ROI: the measurable return (revenue acceleration, cost mitigation) generated by the human capital asset. This re-labels HR from a cost center to a Profit Enabler and forces the CFO to engage with HR's budget as a necessary investment, not discretionary overhead.

Peer Function	The Perceived Threat	The Turf War Is Over...
Operations (VP of Ops)	The Efficiency Threat: HR's initiatives (e.g., mandatory training, standardized performance reviews) are perceived as slowing down production or adding unnecessary process complexity.	Process ownership and velocity, the right to control how work gets done within the function without external interference.
IT (CTO)	The Technology Control Threat: Resistance to HR's push for new HCM/HRIS systems, often viewing HR data as	Data infrastructure and systems, which control the technology backbone, data security, and

Peer Function	The Perceived Threat	The Turf War Is Over...
	secondary or viewing the new system as a security risk under HR's purview.	procurement budget for key systems.

Blueprint for Collaboration: The Case Study

The single case study in this chapter, "The Operations Manager's Resistance (Manufacturing)," is designed to provide a blueprint for neutralizing a classic turf war.

Its purpose is to teach you the most effective counter-tactic: Negotiate Benefits, Not Rules. The Operations VP was debating a process rule ("Your paperwork slows us down"). The HR Director refused to engage in that debate. Instead, she used the Integrator Statement principle by quantifying the financial cost of the VP's preferred autonomous method (high defect and injury rates). You should use this outcome as a model to always pivot the conversation from a subjective process debate (who is right) to an objective financial debate (what costs the business more). This is the only way to secure compliance and recast HR's role as a cost and risk control measure for the peer function.

Case Study: The Operations Manager's Resistance (Manufacturing)

Issue: An HR Director at a $75 million manufacturer introduced a standardized "Candidate Interview Loop" to ensure consistent quality of hire for factory floor technicians (Hiring Autonomy Threat). The VP of Operations immediately resisted, arguing, "We need to hire fast! Your paperwork slows down the floor and costs us production time." The VP was resisting the Efficiency Threat.

Action Taken (Neutralizing with Data): HR did not argue the process, but the cost. The HR Director presented data showing that the technicians hired without the standardized loop had a 60% higher defect rate and a 50% higher on-the-job incident rate in their first six months. The cost of defects and injury claims far outweighed the few hours saved by quick, informal hiring.

Outcome: By quantifying the operational cost of the VP's resistance ($95,000 in recurring costs), HR reframed the standardized process as a risk and cost control measure for the Operations department, securing grudging, then enthusiastic, compliance.

Threat Mapping Matrix

Navigating Executive Concerns in HR Initiatives

Threat Type (Executive Concern)	Typical Reaction (Executive Behavior)	Strategic Counter (HR Approach)
Money (Cost/Profit)	Budget Cuts, Focus on on ROI Short-term View	Quantify HR Impact, Highlight cost savings, Link to revenue
Authority (Control/influence)	Micromanagement, Resistance to Change, Turf Wars	Collaborate early, Share ownership Provide data-driven options
Competence (Skill/Knowledge)	Skepticism, Dismissal of HR Data, Reliance on in ternal	Educate with clear visuals Offer pilot programs internal benchmarks

8.3 The Zero-Sum Fallacy: Becoming the Integrator

The Strategic HR leader must actively and repeatedly debunk the core premise of the turf war: the zero-sum fallacy. The mistaken belief that one person's gain is another's loss. Strategic HR is explicitly about enlarging the pie for everyone by optimizing the human capital asset, which benefits all departments equally. The HR leader's mandate is to act as the ultimate Integrator, demonstrating through clear, quantified communication how HR's success directly benefits the peer function in measurable terms that matter to them (e.g., reduced costs for Finance, increased stability for Operations). This shifts the conversation from departmental control to mutual dependency. HR is not there to police; HR is there to guarantee the stability and high performance of the peer executive's most critical asset: their people.

What It Is: The mistaken belief that HR gaining strategic authority must mean other functional leaders are losing their own power or influence.

Why It's Important for the Business: Debunking this fallacy is crucial for fostering mutual dependency and collaborative goal-setting, thereby breaking down departmental silos that impede the execution of enterprise-wide strategies.

Action: The Integrator Statement

The HR leader's key action is to replace the challenge with a quantified benefit statement. This reframes HR's involvement as a direct operational gain.

- **Example to the VP of Operations (Efficiency Threat):** *Original Resistance:* "Your training takes our supervisors off the floor." Integrator Statement: "Our new manager coaching program reduced regrettable turnover among line supervisors by 20%. This means Operations saved 400 training hours annually on replacement supervisors, directly increasing available production time and reducing your cost of quality checks. Our system guarantees your operational stability."

Chapter 8 Checklist: Understanding the Turf War

Action	Outcome
Action 1: Identify your single biggest peer skeptic (CFO, VP of Ops, etc.).	Pinpoints the most critical relationship requiring immediate strategic attention.
Action 2: Determine the specific **threat** HR poses to their department (metrics, autonomy, or process control).	Provides the necessary context to negotiate a mutually beneficial solution.
Action 3: Draft a "Win-Win" statement debunking the zero-sum fallacy for that peer (e.g., "Our turnover reduction saves Operations 400 training hours annually, directly increasing their available production time").	Creates the opening line for reframing HR's involvement as a benefit, not a burden.

Key Takeaways

- **Friction is Structural:** The turf war is not personal; it's a conflict over control of budget, processes, and data ownership.

- **Identify the Threat:** Understand that the CFO fears losing metric authority, the VP of Ops fears losing efficiency/process control, and the CTO fears losing data infrastructure control.

- **Debunk Zero-Sum:** Act as the **Integrator** by proactively demonstrating that HR's success creates measurable, positive financial and operational benefits for every peer executive.

- **Negotiate Benefits, Not Rules:** Never debate HR rules; only debate the **quantified cost and risk reduction** HR's systems provide to the peer's department.

Reflection

Use these questions to spark discussion with your leadership team.

- What is the single biggest process where a functional leader's historical autonomy (e.g., hiring on instinct) is creating a recurring financial cost for the entire enterprise?

- How can we present our HRIS investment to the CTO as an asset security measure for critical people data, rather than just an HR system?

- If we succeed in reducing regrettable turnover by 10% next quarter, what specific, measurable benefit (e.g., fewer quality checks, lower travel expense) will that translate to for the Sales or Operations VP?

- Which peer executive is currently the most resistant to data sharing, and what data-backed "Integrator Statement" can we create to win them over?

Chapter 9: Building Shared Ownership and Collaboration

Summary

Once the dynamics of the Turf War are understood, the Strategic HR leader's focus shifts to transforming resistance into robust enterprise-wide collaboration. This is achieved by systematically implementing the Co-Pilot Approach, adopting Shared Metrics to enforce mutual accountability, and clearly defining organizational boundaries to preserve peer autonomy, thus building shared ownership of the people strategy.

Step-by-Step Framework

The success of the Strategic HR transformation hinges on its ability to move beyond merely debunking the zero-sum fallacy (Chapter 8) and into a state of robust, enterprise-wide collaboration. This requires a fundamental, systematic shift in HR's operational identity. The function must cease to be perceived as a centralized oversight body, the "policy police," and become a genuine strategic resource provider and integrator. This systematic shift relies on the intentional implementation of shared accountability mechanisms, such as shared metrics and clearly defined organizational boundaries, that transform peer friction into necessary cooperation. The ultimate goal is to embed the people strategy so deeply into the business that the functional leader views its success as inseparable from their own.

Co-Pilot Accounability Model

Joint Ownership for Shared Success

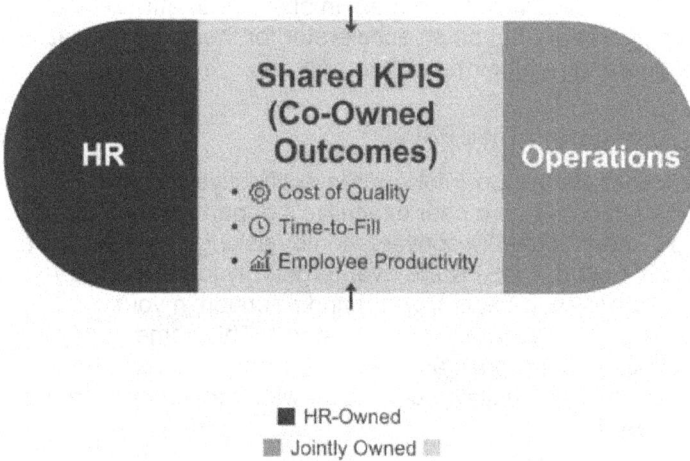

HR

Shared KPIS (Co-Owned Outcomes)
- ◎ Cost of Quality
- ◷ Time-to-Fill
- ⚏ Employee Productivity

Operations

■ HR-Owned
▨ Jointly Owned ▨

Discussion: To permanently neutralize the perceived threat of HR imposing rules from above, the strategic leader must fundamentally reposition the function to a Co-Pilot Approach. This requires a deliberate and sustained effort to lead with service and support. When engaging with a department head (like the VP of Sales or the CTO), the HR leader must explicitly frame their job as providing the talent data, development resources, and structural support necessary for the peer leader to meet their specific operational and financial goals. By shifting the language away from antagonistic terms like "mandate," "compliance," or "policy requirement" toward collaborative language like "joint priority," "mutual objective," and "integrated strategy," HR immediately lowers the peer's defensiveness, establishes a foundation of mutual trust, and cultivates a sense of dependency. The HR leader becomes an internal consultant whose expertise is explicitly focused on accelerating the peer's departmental success.

What It Is: The deliberate act of positioning HR as a supportive resource partner whose primary goal is enabling the functional leader to achieve their own, non-HR operational and financial targets. HR does not own the goal; it partners on the strategy to achieve it.

Why It's Important for the Business: This approach replaces territorial resistance with a mindset of service, ensuring functional leaders view HR not as an obstacle to efficiency (the Efficiency Threat), but as an accelerator for their own success and a guarantor of their team's stability.

Lead by Analyzing Their P&L

To demonstrate the Co-Pilot Approach effectively, spend 30 minutes analyzing your peer executive's departmental P&L or budget. Then, begin the conversation by asking: "I see your Cost of Goods Sold (COGS) is 2% over target; my job is to help you fix that by ensuring better training and retention in your production roles. Where should we start?" This immediately establishes your purpose as a financial partner, not an administrator, and aligns your support with their primary area of accountability.

Blueprint for Collaboration: The Case Study

The single case study in this chapter, Shared Metrics Neutralize the CFO (Tech), is designed to provide a definitive blueprint for resolving the Budget Control Threat using the principle of Shared Metrics.

The purpose of this case study is to prove that financial accountability is a more powerful motivator for collaboration than any amount of internal HR policy or debate. The CFO only collaborated when his bonus was tied to the metric HR controlled. You should use the outcome as a direct model for resolving your own turf wars with the Finance or Operations teams. By proposing a Shared Metric that links your talent efficiency (e.g., Time-to-Fill, training quality) to your peer's financial performance (e.g., revenue opportunity, quality cost), you transform resistance into mutual financial dependency.

9.2 Shared Metrics: Enforcing Collaboration

Discussion: The most powerful tactical tool for dismantling departmental silos and eliminating turf wars is the implementation of Shared Metrics. These are Key Performance Indicators (KPIs) that are designed to require two or more functional leaders, including HR, to collaborate and succeed together, linking their individual accountabilities to a single enterprise outcome. This mechanism makes failure a shared financial burden, thus transforming functional friction into necessary cooperation.

What It Is: Key Performance Indicators that are tracked and owned jointly by HR and one or more peer leaders, linking their success to a unified business outcome and preventing one function from optimizing its performance at the expense of another.

Shared Metric Examples

Metric	Departments Owning It	Financial Goal Impacted
Customer acquisition cost	Marketing and Sales	Profitability
Lead conversion rate	Customer Success and Marketing	Revenue growth
Customer churn rate	Customer Success and Support	Customer retention
Net promoter score	Sales and Finance	Revenue growth
Sales revenue		Revenue growth

Why It's Important for the Business: Shared Metrics force collaboration and ensure that the pursuit of one department's goal (e.g., Operations chasing lower labor cost) does not inadvertently sabotage another's (e.g., HR struggling with high retention costs due to understaffing), aligning functional effort toward enterprise value.

Examples of Shared Metrics

- **Cost of Quality (Operations and HR):** This metric tracks the total financial cost associated with manufacturing defects, rework, and warranty claims. Operations owns the process and equipment maintenance, but HR owns the rigor of the training, certification, and staffing levels for the technicians. If quality fails, both are equally accountable, forcing joint ownership of the training and staffing solutions.

- **Strategic Initiative Time-to-Market (R&D, Sales, and HR):** This metric tracks the time elapsed from project approval to product launch. HR owns securing the specialized talent for the project (Talent Acquisition/Forecasting), R&D owns the development cycle, and Sales owns market preparedness. HR's metric success (Time-to-Hire) directly impacts the Sales team's revenue goal, forcing them to collaborate on candidate profiles and interview prioritization.

- **Absenteeism Cost (Finance, Operations, and HR):** While HR owns the policies, Finance tracks the cost of covering absent workers, and Operations tracks the reduction in productive hours. All three are jointly accountable for driving the cost down.

Case Study: Shared Metrics Neutralize the CFO (Tech)

Issue: The CFO at a $100 million software company consistently blocked HR initiatives, viewing them only as cost increases (The Budget Control Threat). HR's recruiting team was slow, but the CFO refused to approve a higher-cost recruiting software.

Action Taken (Implementing Shared Metrics): HR did not argue for the software; they argued for a Shared Metric: "Time-to-Fill Critical Roles," which they jointly owned with the CFO. HR proposed that the metric's performance would directly impact on both HR's efficiency bonus and the CFO's budget adherence bonus. They established the baseline Time-to-Fill was 90 days.

Intervention and Outcome: Within one quarter, the shared metric quickly showed that the 90-day Time-to-Fill was causing $40,000 in lost revenue opportunity for the Sales team. Because the CFO's bonus was now tied to the failing metric, the resistance vanished. The CFO quickly partnered with HR to approve the higher-cost recruiting software and fund a dedicated recruiter, viewing the expense not as a cost, but as a necessary investment to fix his failing metric and secure his bonus. The turf war was replaced by mutual financial accountability.

9.3 Defining Boundaries: Guardrails, Not Micromanagement

Discussion: Lack of clarity is a leading source of conflict and peer resistance. Functional leaders become resistant (the Autonomy Threat) when they fear HR will micromanage their day-to-day operations. To prevent this, the HR leader must clearly communicate and document a documented division of labor, what HR will and will not control. HR's strategic territory should be centralized, focusing on the "why" and the "what" of people management (e.g., compensation philosophy, standardized recruiting process design, talent forecasting). The functional leader's territory should be decentralized, focusing on the "how" (e.g., day-to-day scheduling, individual employee project priorities, specific coaching techniques). The principle is simple: HR should act as a guardrail on strategic decisions, ensuring enterprise consistency and risk mitigation, but should not interfere with the operational details the manager is paid to execute.

What It Is: Clear documentation and communication detailing the division of labor between centralized HR authority (the strategic framework) and decentralized managerial autonomy (the operational execution).

Why It's Important for the Business: Clarity drastically reduces conflict and minimizes the perception of bureaucratic interference, which preserves the functional leader's essential ownership and accountability for their daily operations.

9.4 Cross-Functional HR: The HR Business Partner as Integrator

Crossfunctional Performance Gains

Performance Improvement Post Shared-Ownership Implemeñation

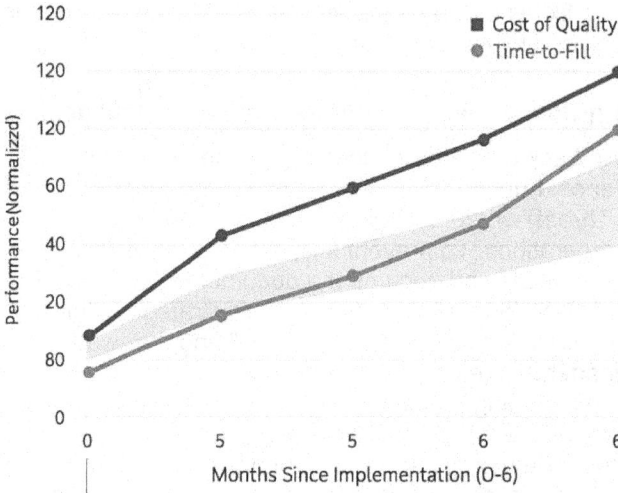

Legend:
- Cost of Quality
- Time-to-Fill

Y-axis (Performance(Normalizzd)): 0, 80, 20, 40, 60, 120, 120, 120

X-axis (Months Since Implementation (0-6)): 0, 5, 5, 6, 6

The proper implementation of the HR Business Partner (HRBP) model is essential for executing a strategic approach and serving as the physical manifestation of the Co-Pilot Approach. For this model to succeed, the HRBP must navigate a critical organizational dualism: they must maintain a solid-line reporting structure to the central HR function (to ensure data standardization, legal compliance, and consistent policy adherence) while simultaneously operating with a deep, advisory partnership with the functional leader. This requires the HRBP to immerse themselves in the operational details of the department they support, becoming proficient in that department's business objectives (e.g., understanding the sales funnel or the engineering sprint process). This deep operational context ensures that HR recommendations are always grounded in operational reality and are directly relevant to the peer leader's execution challenges. The HRBP thus acts as the bridge and integrator, linking centralized strategy to decentralized execution.

What It Is: The deployment of HR professionals who report centrally but are embedded as strategic, operationally aware advisors within a specific business unit, possessing business acumen equal to their HR expertise.

Why It's Important for the Business: It ensures that the overall HR strategy is executed consistently across the enterprise, while providing personalized, operationally informed talent support to functional leaders, thereby accelerating problem resolution and enhancing the quality of people-related decision-making.

Chapter 9 Checklist: Building Shared Ownership

Action	Outcome
Action 1: Reframe your role using "**Co-Pilot**" language in all executive interactions: "My job is to support your business goals and guarantee your team's stability."	Transformation of territorial resistance into a service-oriented partnership.
Action 2: Initiate a "**Shared Metrics**" conversation with one key peer leader, proposing joint accountability for a key business outcome (e.g., Cost of Quality or Time-to-Market).	The first step toward establishing mutual dependency and dismantling functional silos.
Action 3: Document clear **boundaries** on what HR controls (strategic decision frameworks) versus what the manager controls (day-to-day execution).	Reduction of conflict by preserving the functional leader's essential operational autonomy.

Key Takeaways

- **Co-Pilot, Not Police:** HR must lead with service, positioning itself as a resource partner dedicated to achieving the peer executive's functional goals.

- **Force Collaboration: Shared Metrics** are the most powerful tool for ending turf wars, as they financially link the success of HR (e.g., training) to the success of the peer (e.g., reduced defect rate).

- **Clarity Prevents Conflict:** Explicitly defining the boundaries between centralized HR authority (the **what**) and managerial autonomy (the **how**) preserves the manager's operational ownership.

- **HRBP as Integrator:** The HR Business Partner must be an operationally astute professional who acts as the bridge between centralized HR strategy and decentralized business execution.

Reflection

Use these questions to spark discussion with your leadership team.

- What is the biggest operational bottleneck in the company right now, and how can HR jointly own a metric with the responsible peer executive to force a collaborative solution?

- Where are our current organizational boundaries most blurred, and how is that lack of clarity causing specific, documented conflict between HR and a functional department?

- If we audited the time the VP of Operations spends managing people problems, what dollar cost of their time could we save by deploying a strong HR Business Partner as a Co-Pilot?

- What specific incentive (e.g., lower budget oversight, accelerated project funding) can we offer a resistant peer executive in exchange for agreeing to a Shared Metric?

Chapter 10: The Art of the Collaborative Win

Summary

Achieving strategic influence requires continuous, positive human interaction. This chapter provides tactical guidance for institutionalizing collaboration by leading with service, practicing credit sharing to reduce peer insecurity, and Formalizing Partnerships through joint committees. The goal is to build a history of reciprocity that makes peer leaders eager to partner with HR on all strategic initiatives.

Step-by-Step Framework

Strategic influence requires more than just formal systems; it demands continuous, positive human interaction. Chapter 10 focuses on the social currency of executive leadership: trust, credit, and mutual gain. The ultimate success of the Strategic HR leader lies not just in designing perfect policies, but in transforming former functional resistance (Chapter 8) into a powerful, institutionalized alliance. This transformation hinges on building a history of positive, service-oriented interactions that make peers eager to partner with HR on the next strategic initiative, replacing mandatory compliance with willing collaboration.

10.1 Leading with Service: Building Reciprocal Trust

The most effective and immediate way to disarm a skeptical peer, the executive who still views HR as the "policy police," is to proactively solve one of their most urgent, non-HR-mandated problems. This tactic, known as Leading with Service, strategically establishes HR as a dedicated problem-solver and resource partner whose commitment transcends the official HR mandate. For instance, if the VP of Operations is struggling to model complex logistics schedules, the HR leader can offer the support of a skilled HR analyst to build the models. This calculated act of service builds deep trust and creates significant political capital. When HR eventually requires cooperation on its own strategic initiatives (e.g., standardizing hiring processes or implementing shared metrics), the peer leader is already indebted to the partnership, making compliance significantly easier to secure. This is reciprocity put into action.

Influence Ladder

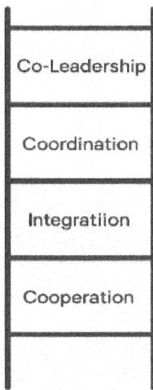

Co-Leadership
Coordination
Integratiion
Cooperation

What It Is: Proactively identifying and solving a peer leader's most pressing business problem, even if the task falls slightly outside of HR's formal mandate (e.g., providing data analysis for a marketing structure or modeling an operations budget).

Why It's Important for the Business: It establishes a foundation of reciprocity and trust with skeptical peers. By demonstrating competence in solving operational problems, HR validates its place as a valued, multidisciplinary partner across the enterprise, accelerating the pace of organizational change.

Common Mistake – Becoming the Departmental Janitor

The critical error in Leading with Service is allowing the HR function to become an on-demand administrative service for other departments. If the VP of Sales starts asking HR to format their spreadsheets or compile their weekly reports, HR has failed. The Service must be a strategic, one-time intervention that solves a high-level structural problem (e.g., organizational design), not a recurring operational burden (e.g., data entry). Strategic service builds capacity; administrative service drains it.

Blueprint for Influence: The Case Study

The single case study in this chapter, Organizational Design Support (Marketing), provides the definitive example of the Leading with Service strategy.

The purpose of this case study is to prove that political capital is a necessary prerequisite for structural change. The Marketing VP was resistant to HR's policies due to a lack of trust. HR did not argue about the policy; they solved the VP's unrelated, internal operational pain (disorganized structure). You should use this outcome as a model to demonstrate how a calculated act of high-value, non-mandated service can instantly eliminate a peer's skepticism and transform them into an internal champion for your next major strategic initiative (such as changing the performance review cycle).

**Case Example: Organizational Design Support (Marketing)
The Strategic Turnaround**

Issue: The VP of Marketing was struggling with high internal friction due to a confusing, disorganized employee structure, hindering campaign launch speed. The VP, lacking expertise in organizational design, felt overwhelmed and viewed HR with suspicion due to prior policy conflicts.

Action Taken (Service Intervention): The HR Director executed the Leading with Service strategy. The Director offered to dedicate an HR analyst, a professional skilled in data modeling and organizational structure, to model three alternative organizational design options for the VP of Marketing. This was a non-mandated service focused entirely on solving the VP's operational problem, saving him time and budget while delivering expert solutions.

Actual Outcome: The VP of Marketing, relieved by the expert, data-driven support, fully accepted one of the organizational models. When HR later proposed a mandatory, company-wide change to the performance review cycle (a process change the VP previously resisted), the VP of Marketing not only accepted it but became its strongest internal champion, citing the expert support they received from HR as the reason for their newfound trust.

10.2 Credit Sharing: Investing in Peer Insecurity

In the executive world, credit is a powerful, non-monetary currency that must be managed strategically. When a shared initiative succeeds (e.g., reduced regrettable turnover in the Operations department due to HR-designed training), the strategic HR leader must intentionally ensure the functional peer leader receives the lion's share of the public and executive-level praise. This tactic, known as Credit Sharing or Strategic Praise, directly addresses and reduces the peer's underlying insecurity (Chapter 8). By allowing the peer to claim victory, reporting the metric to the CEO as their own achievement, HR makes them feel valued, competent, and protected from the perceived "data threat." This act of Strategic Praise costs the HR leader nothing, yet generates enormous goodwill, transforming the peer from a reluctant participant into an enthusiastic and eager collaborator on future projects. By giving away credit for the small wins, HR ultimately gains influence over the entire strategic portfolio.

What It Is: Intentionally directing most of the public and executive-level praise for a shared success (like improved productivity or reduced risk) to the peer leader who executed the plan.

Why It's Important for the Business: It lowers the peer's defensiveness and transforms collaboration from a mandatory process into a personally rewarding experience for the peer, effectively guaranteeing their enthusiastic cooperation on future, larger initiatives.

10.3 Formalizing Partnerships: Institutionalizing Influence

While leading with Service and Credit Sharing builds personal trust, Formalizing Partnerships institutionalizes that collaboration, making HR's influence structural and non-negotiable. This involves establishing joint leadership steering committees that meet regularly (e.g., monthly). The agenda priority for these committees must be explicitly focused on the business strategy first (e.g., "Review Q3 Sales Targets") and then the resulting talent implications ("Do we have the people, skills, and organizational design to hit those targets?"). This structure ensures that HR is not only present during strategic planning but also familiarizes peer leaders with discussing talent as a joint, strategic asset, thereby embedding HR's influence into the core decision-making structure of the business. The goal is to make the joint planning committee the natural and necessary forum for all major strategic decisions involving people or organizational design.

What It Is: Institutionalizing collaboration by establishing joint leadership committees (e.g., a "Talent Steering Committee" or "Operational Readiness Committee") whose primary agenda is reviewing business strategy and subsequent talent implications.

Credit-Sharing Framework
Joint Recognition for Collaborative Success

Action	Partner(s)	Credit Allocation (%)
Implemented Automated Onboarding	HR & IT	HR: 60%, IT 40%
Reduced Cost-to-Fill by 15%	HR & Operations	HR: 70%, Operations: 30%
Launched Leadership Development Program	HR & Executive Team	HR: 50%, Executive Team:

Why It's Important for the Business: This mechanism ensures HR hears business strategy before it's executed, allowing for proactive talent planning (Gap Analysis, Buy/Build/Borrow decisions) and ensuring talent constraints are addressed early, rather than late, when they can derail major initiatives and lead to expensive panic-hiring.

Chapter 10 Checklist: Collaborative Win

Action	Outcome
Action 1: Identify one non-HR-mandated problem for your most skeptical peer and offer a service-oriented solution (e.g., organizational design support).	Building a foundation of trust and reciprocity.
Action 2: In your next executive update, practice Strategic Praise by directing the majority of the credit for a shared success (e.g., lower TTTP) to your peer.	Reduced peer insecurity and guaranteed eagerness for future partnerships.
Action 3: Propose creating a joint leadership steering committee with 2-3 key peers to review	Institutionalization of collaboration and HR's strategic influence.

Action	Outcome
business strategy and talent implications monthly.	

Key Takeaways

- **Lead with Reciprocity:** Build trust by proactively leading with Service to solve a peer's non-HR problem, creating political capital for future cooperation.

- **Credit is Influence:** Practice Credit Sharing by intentionally giving public praise to peer executives for shared successes, which transforms resistance into enthusiastic advocacy.

- **Formalize Influence:** Formalize Partnerships through joint committees whose primary mandate is reviewing business strategy, ensuring HR's voice is structurally embedded in core decision-making.

- **Institutionalize Collaboration:** Build a history of positive, service-oriented interactions to replace compliance with mutual dependency.

Reflection

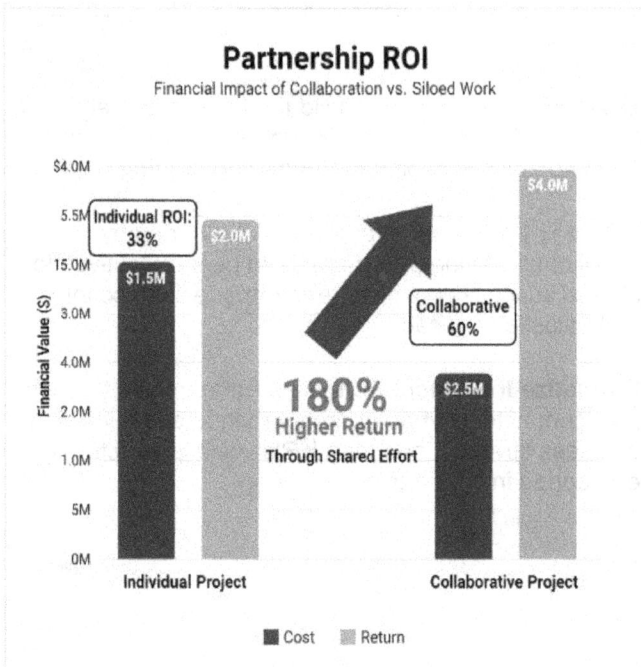

Partnership ROI

Financial Impact of Collaboration vs. Siloed Work

Use these questions to spark discussion with your leadership team.

- Which peer executive is most likely to be susceptible to the Leading with Service tactic, and what is one non-HR problem we could solve for them within 30 days?

- If we audited our recent successes, where did we fail to practice Credit Sharing, and how did that missed opportunity impact the willingness of that peer to partner again?

- What 1-2 key business goals must be on the agenda of our new joint steering committee to ensure its meetings are always viewed as strategic, not administrative?

- How can we use the success of a collaborative win to propose a Shared Metric with a peer executive, ensuring the next win is structurally guaranteed?

Chapter 11: Developing the Strategic HR Team

Summary

The final stage of strategic transformation requires the HR leader to transform the team itself. This involves shifting the team's identity from policy processors to business consultants by demanding new competencies in financial acumen, business strategy, and predictive analytics. This internal evolution is institutionalized through a formal Competency Model and a proactive recruiting strategy that prioritizes candidates with non-HR operational experience.

Step-by-Step Framework

The primary and most enduring responsibility of the Strategic HR leader is internal: ensuring the HR department itself is fit for its new purpose. Strategic HR is not a policy manual; it is the collective mindset and capability of the team. The team must undergo a radical identity shift, moving from a group of administrative processors and policy enforcers to a team of business consultants who use data to drive enterprise-level decisions. This transition requires a fundamental and non-negotiable change in skill sets, moving away from clerical compliance (e.g., manually filing documents) toward competencies directly tied to business financial health (e.g., ROI calculation and risk mitigation). If the HR team fails to evolve its skills, the strategic shift will inevitably fail, as new systems will simply be managed with an old, tactical mindset, making the strategic function a façade.

11.1 Shifting Skill Sets: From Process to Prediction

The move to strategic HR is a professional evolution for everyone on the team, demanding a different way of thinking and communicating. Training must prioritize building business acumen, understanding the company's financial model, competitive market, and operational value chain, over securing traditional, siloed HR certifications. Tactical skills remain essential for the daily maintenance of the firm, but they are wholly insufficient for strategy. The team needs to learn how to move beyond historical reporting (what happened last quarter) to predictive analytics (what will happen next year) and consultative communication, engaging managers as internal clients and measuring their own success by business outcome, not process completion.

The Strategic Skill Transition

From (Tactical Skill)	To (Strategic Capability)	What This Means for the Business
Policy Enforcement	**Risk and Compliance Advisor**	Moving from reacting to violations to proactively anticipating and mitigating high-cost legal, ethical, and safety exposure across the enterprise.
Payroll Processing	**HR Technology and Automation Expert**	Managing technology platforms (HRIS/HCM) to drive efficiency, standardize workflows, and guarantee the clean, reliable data necessary for strategic reporting.
Interview Scheduling	**Talent Strategy and Forecasting Analyst**	Using predictive data to anticipate future skill gaps, identifying critical roles, and designing proactive, multi-year recruiting pipelines (Buy, Build, Borrow).
Document Filing	**Change Management Consultant**	Leading organizational shifts (like implementing new performance systems or organizational restructures) to ensure successful adoption, manager buy-in, and measurable business impact.

The Job Shadowing Exchange

To rapidly build Operational Context within your existing team, institute a mandatory, one-week, internal "Job Shadowing Exchange." Have an HR Business Partner spend a week embedded in the Operations department, and in return, have an Operations manager spend a week with the HR team. This cross-functional immersion costs almost nothing but forces the HR team to gain first-hand understanding of the value chain, the production bottlenecks, and the true pain points that drive the P&L.

Blueprint for Team Evolution: The Case Study

The single case study in this chapter, Hiring for Business Acumen (SaaS), provides the definitive evidence that non-HR expertise accelerates strategic impact.

The purpose of this case study is to prove that financial literacy is a skill gap you must fill with external talent if it cannot be developed internally. The old HR team failed because they lacked the operational context to calculate a believable ROI. The new, non-traditional hire succeeded because they immediately implemented a business-relevant metric (reduction in technical support calls) that translated directly into a quantifiable financial gain ($50,000 savings). You should use the outcome as a model to challenge your own recruitment biases and to justify prioritizing a candidate's P&L understanding and business acumen over deep, traditional HR policy knowledge.

11.2 The Competency Model: The Blueprint for Success

Strategic HR Competency Model

Defining the Modern HR Business Partner

Competency	Behavioral Example	Business Outcome
Business Acumen & Financial Literacy	Connects HR initiatives to financial statements	Increased ROI,
Data-Driven Decision Making	Uses workforce analytics to predict turnovor risks	Improved Taient Forecasting Proactive Solutions
Strategic & Systems Thinking	Designs HR strategies that support long-term growth	Sustainable Growth, Organizational Retilience

To make the strategic shift permanent and sustainable, the HR leader must develop a formal:

Competency Model for the function. This model is the blueprint for how the HR team operates, serving as the non-negotiable standard for recruiting, training, and rewarding HR professionals. The model must clearly signal the new requirements of the job, that technical HR expertise is secondary to business-driving skills. Critically, this model must include competencies traditionally found outside the HR function.

Financial Acumen (the ability to read a P&L statement and calculate ROI) and

Business Strategy (understanding the company's competitive position, target market, and operational goals). This formal structure institutionalizes the function's new strategic purpose and ensures every team member knows they are measured on their ability to deliver financial impact.

What It Is: A formal, documented framework outlining the specific, non-traditional business and financial skills required for success in the strategic HR function.

Why It's Important for the Business: It institutionalizes the new identity of HR, ensuring that future hires and internal development efforts align precisely with the executive demand for data, financial literacy, and strategic decision support.

11.3 Recruiting for the Future: Hiring the Business Mindset

The fastest way to transform the HR team's collective capability is through strategic hiring. When recruiting for HR positions, the strategic leader must proactively prioritize candidates with demonstrated experience outside of a traditional HR silo. The core insight here is that HR expertise can be taught; business acumen and strategic thinking are much harder to cultivate. Targeting candidates with backgrounds in Finance, Operations, or Consulting brings an immediate business-first perspective and crucial financial literacy to the HR team. These individuals are already fluent in the language of the C-Suite, accelerating the entire function's ability to communicate strategic value. This intentional hiring practice ensures the team is equipped to handle complex strategic challenges from day one, injecting much-needed operational and financial credibility into the department.

What It Is: Prioritizing candidates with demonstrated experience in operations, finance, or consulting roles during the HR recruitment process, specifically valuing their P&L perspective over deep policy knowledge.

Why It's Important for the Business: It immediately elevates the quality of business judgment within the HR team, accelerating the function's transition to a strategic consultancy and improving the rigor of all internal ROI analyses.

Case Study: Hiring for Business Acumen (SaaS) The Strategic Turnaround

Issue: The HR team at a $150 million SaaS company struggled to justify its $30,000 annual training budget, consistently failing to calculate a believable ROI for the CFO. The team had high policy knowledge but zero financial context.

Action Taken (Strategic Recruiting): The HR Director implemented a new competency model, which requires Financial Acumen for all new hires. The Director then intentionally recruited a new HR Manager who had spent three years in a project management and operations role and lacked a traditional HR background. The hiring pitch was: "We will teach you HR law; you will teach us how the business makes money."

Outcome: Within six months, the new manager used her operational background to redesign the technical training program. She implemented a new metric that tracked the reduction in technical support calls from the field sales team after the training. This reduction translated directly into $50,000 in calculated savings for the IT department, proving a clear 1.6x ROI on the training budget. The new manager's operational perspective immediately succeeded where the old team's pure-HR focus had failed, securing the training budget permanently.

Chapter 11 Checklist: Developing the Strategic HR Team

Action	Outcome
Action 1: Map your team's current skills to the Strategic Capabilities table and identify the top three gaps in Business Acumen and Financial Literacy.	A clear training plan and recruitment roadmap for professional development.
Action 2: Initiate cross-training on basic business finance and metrics (Month 3 action) for all existing HR staff, focusing on how to read the company's P&L statement.	Development of core Financial Acumen within the team.
Action 3: Update job descriptions for all open HR roles to specifically require experience or demonstrated competency in business operations or	Transformation of the HR department into business consultants.

Action	Outcome
finance, prioritizing this over traditional HR certifications.	

Key Takeaways

- **Evolve the Team:** Strategic HR requires a fundamental identity shift from policy processor to business consultant and problem-solver.

- **Competency is Financial:** Institute a formal Competency Model that prioritizes Financial Acumen and Business Strategy over traditional HR technical skills.

- **Hire Outside the Silo:** Proactively recruit candidates with backgrounds in **Finance, Operations, or Consulting** to inject business-first thinking and financial literacy into the team.

- **Measure Strategy:** Success must be measured by the business outcome (ROI, cost reduction) the team delivers, not the number of processes completed.

Cross-Functional Hiring Impact

Project ROI Before & After Interdisciplinary Hires

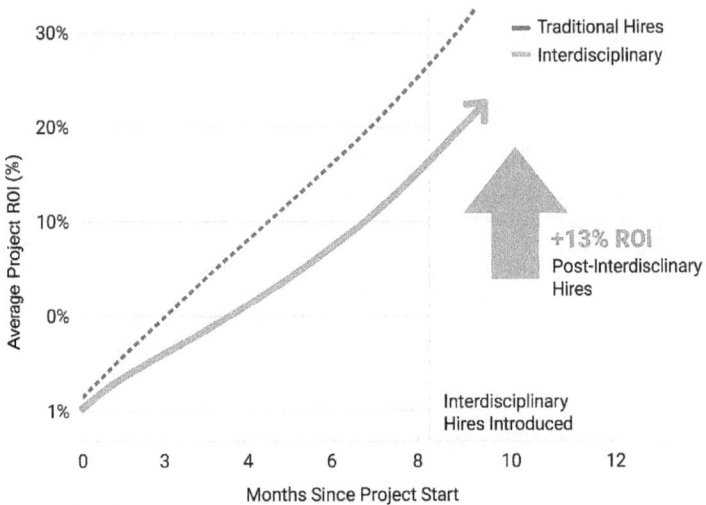

+13% ROI
Post-Interdisclinary Hires

Interdisciplinary Hires Introduced

Legend:
— Traditional Hires
— Interdisciplinary

Y-axis: Average Project ROI (%) — 1%, 0%, 10%, 20%, 30%
X-axis: Months Since Project Start — 0, 3, 4, 6, 8, 10, 12

Reflection

Use these questions to spark discussion with your leadership team.

- If we hired a non-HR professional for our next open HR role, what specific operational problem could their experience solve that our current team cannot?

- What is the single biggest, recurring business cost that our HR team does not currently understand well enough to analyze and propose a solution for?

- Does our current HR team's performance review system reward compliance or reward quantifiable business impact?

- What training investment is necessary to ensure every HR professional can confidently calculate the ROI of their last major project?

Chapter 12: Continuous Measurement and Adaptation

Summary

A true strategic function is dynamic; it adapts constantly. This chapter outlines the formal governance required for continuous adaptation, including the Quarterly Strategic Review to maintain executive accountability, Scenario Planning to manage talent risk, and systemic Feedback Loops to ensure the HR strategy remains highly relevant and responsive to market and organizational shifts.

Step-by-Step Framework

A true strategic function is fundamentally dynamic; it does not set a plan and rigidly follow it regardless of external conditions. Instead, it measures results, learns from new data, and adapts its strategy continuously. This final phase, Continuous Measurement and Adaptation, outlines the formal governance structures necessary to ensure the HR strategy remains a relevant, high-value asset amidst the constant shifts in market conditions, disruptive technology, and organizational goals. By institutionalizing regular review and predictive modeling, the HR

Quarterly Review Template

Tracking HR's Strategic Impact

Metric	Current Value	Target	Next-Step Action
Time-to-Fill	45 days	30 days	
			Streamline interview process
Turnovr Cost	$1.2M	$800K	Enhance exit/stay interviews
Employee Engagement	68%	80%	Launch leadership training

function transforms into the organization's chief risk manager for talent, a permanent and indispensable strategic role.

12.1 The Quarterly Strategic Review: Sustaining Accountability

To ensure the hard-won alignment achieved in previous phases is sustained, the HR leader must formally mandate a Quarterly Strategic Review with the executive leadership team. This meeting is fundamentally different from administrative updates or quarterly business reviews (QBRs) that cover all departments. The Strategic Review is dedicated solely to reviewing the measurable impact of the HR strategy against the predetermined, high-level business goals agreed upon in the Alignment Workshop (Chapter 4). The conversation must be focused entirely on quantitative performance and financial results, not internal HR effort. Questions focus on business outcomes: *Did the Time-to-Productivity (TTTP) metric improve, accelerating revenue recognition? Did the targeted retention program save the projected Cost of Regrettable Turnover?* This rigorous, data-driven process prevents "strategy drift" (where the function gradually loses alignment) and maintains executive focus on talent outcomes as a core driver of financial performance.

What It Is: A formal, disciplined quarterly meeting focused exclusively on reviewing measurable HR impact against pre-approved financial and business goals, based on the Executive Scorecard metrics.

Why It's Important for the Business: It provides the mechanism for sustained accountability, holding the executive team accountable for funding talent strategy and holding HR accountable for delivering measurable financial results. It ensures the HR strategy remains agile and responsive to shifting business priorities.

Step-by-Step Action: Executing the Strategic Review

1. **Define the Metrics (Before Meeting):** Select 3-5 Executive Scorecard metrics (e.g., Succession

Readiness Score, TTTP, Cost of Regrettable Turnover) that directly link to the current corporate goal.

2. **Report the Financial Delta:** Present the current metric data alongside the established baseline and the resulting financial delta (the dollars saved, earned, or lost). *Example: "TTTP improved from 12 weeks to 9 weeks, generating $150,000 in accelerated Q3 revenue."*

3. **Propose the Pivot:** Based on the results, propose necessary strategic adjustments. If a program fails, state the data showing the failure and propose a low-cost PoC to fix it. If a program succeeds, propose the company-wide rollout.

12.2 Scenario Planning: Chief Talent Risk Manager

Strategic HR must act as the organization's chief risk manager for talent, looking beyond the next quarter to prepare for market volatility. This requires using People Analytics to model various future scenarios that could disrupt the workforce and quantify the potential financial devastation of each. By modeling potential crises (e.g., a major competitor rapidly hiring away top engineers, a market downturn forcing a reduction in force, or a sudden technology shift making a key skill obsolete), HR can quantify the financial impact of each scenario (e.g., $5 million in severance costs, 18-month delay in product launch). This modeling transforms HR from a reactive service provider into an essential contingency planning unit, demonstrating foresight and actively protecting the company from sudden, catastrophic talent loss or skills obsolescence.[1]

What It Is: Using predictive data (People Analytics) to model potential future crises and develop proactive, quantified workforce contingency plans for both high-growth and high-contraction scenarios.

Why It's Important for the Business: This provides necessary foresight, enabling the executive team to ethically and efficiently manage talent during periods of high risk, such as economic downturns or the adoption of disruptive technology, thereby minimizing the financial shock of external events.

Scenario Planning Readiness Index

Evaluating Organizational Agility for Future HR Challenges

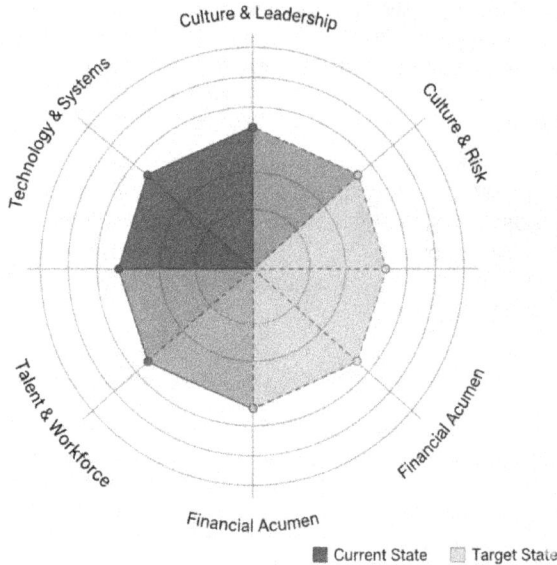

Culture & Leadership
Culture & Systems
Technology & Systems
Culture & Risk
Talent & Workforce
Financial Acumen
Financial Acumen

■ Current State ▨ Target State

Case Study: Economic Downturn Scenario (FinTech)

Issue: A $200 million FinTech firm anticipated a 30% chance of a severe economic downturn within 18 months, requiring a 15% reduction in staff (a necessary Risk Mitigation). Leadership feared the reduction would disproportionately affect key, high-performing engineering teams due to existing salary bands.

Action Taken (Scenario Planning): HR used People Analytics to model two scenarios: 1) a blanket 15% cut (easy but high-risk) and 2) a targeted 15% cut based on *Critical Role analysis* and performance data. The modeling showed that the blanket cut would result in the firm losing 70% of its top-tier engineering talent, costing the firm $2 million in severance and $12 million in lost project revenue. The targeted cut preserved 95% of critical roles while achieving the 15% headcount reduction.

Outcome: The HR-led scenario planning provided the financial evidence to convince the CEO to implement the highly targeted, lower-risk reduction plan, preserving the firm's long-term product

Strategic Feedback Loop

Continuous HR Strategy Optimization

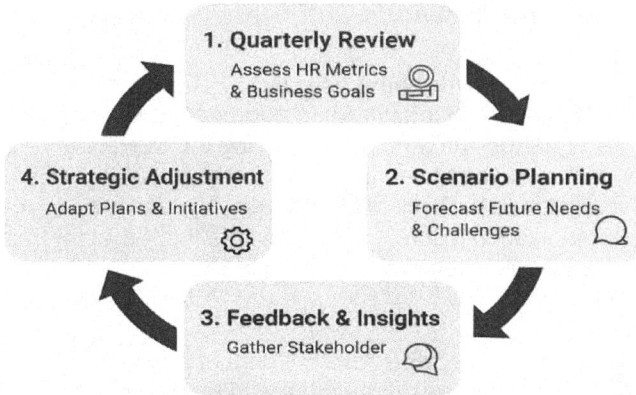

1. Quarterly Review
Assess HR Metrics
& Business Goals

2. Scenario Planning
Forecast Future Needs
& Challenges

3. Feedback & Insights
Gather Stakeholder

4. Strategic Adjustment
Adapt Plans & Initiatives

capabilities and saving the company from a projected $12 million revenue loss. HR was recognized as the chief planning partner in the financial risk management process.

12.3 Feedback Loops: Grounding Strategy in Reality

Discussion: A successful strategic talent strategy must be constantly informed by ground truth, the actual realities of employee and managerial experiences. Feedback Loops provide this continuous stream of qualitative and quantitative data, ensuring HR is not operating in a vacuum. Exit Interviews are critical, as they provide unfiltered data from voluntary departures that often reveal systemic cultural or management failures causing regrettable turnover.[2] This is data the incumbent manager cannot skew. Periodically seeking direct feedback on HR's performance from peer leaders (Executive Perception Audits) ensures the strategy remains precisely aligned with the evolving needs and priorities of the business partners, reinforcing the Co-Pilot relationship.

What It Is: Systematic processes (like exit interviews and executive audits) for gathering continuous, real-world data about the effectiveness and perception of the talent strategy.

Why It's Important for the Business: It ensures the strategic HR function is not operating on assumptions, providing critical, unbiased data to identify and fix systemic problems that lead to costly talent loss and misaligned strategy.

Essential Feedback Loops

1. **Systemic Exit Interview Analysis:** HR must move beyond individual interviews to aggregate the data. Every quarter, run a report identifying the top three systemic reasons cited for voluntary, regrettable departures (e.g., "lack of career path," "manager communication failure"). This provides the target for the next strategic intervention (e.g., a manager coaching program).

2. **Executive Perception Audit:** Conduct anonymous, structured interviews or surveys with key peer executives (CFO, VP Ops, CTO), asking them to rate HR's performance on strategic value (e.g., "How effectively does HR manage talent risk?"). This provides the critical data needed to refine the Co-Pilot approach and immediately address any peer resistance.

Chapter 12 Checklist: Continuous Adaptation

- **Action 1:** Schedule the first Quarterly Strategic Review with the executive team, focusing the agenda solely on the financial results of the Executive Scorecard metrics.

    - **Outcome:** Formalization of the accountability structure and prevention of strategy drift.

- **Action 2:** Model two **Talent Risk Scenarios** (e.g., market downturn and technology shift) and quantify the financial impact of each scenario on revenue and cost.

    - **Outcome:** HR becomes the chief talent risk manager with a proactive contingency plan.

- **Action 3:** Implement an "Exit Interview Data" report to identify the top three systemic management or cultural failures causing regrettable turnover.

- Outcome: Actionable data for solving costly, recurring organizational problems.

Key Takeaways

- **Review Drives Accountability:** The Quarterly Strategic Review is mandatory for sustaining alignment, requiring HR to report business impact, not activity.

- **HR as Risk Manager: Scenario Planning** uses predictive analytics to quantify the financial risk of talent disruption, elevating HR to a contingency planning unit.

- **Truth from Feedback:** Exit Interviews and Executive Perception Audits provide ground truth, ensuring the strategy is constantly informed by the reality of the employee and manager experience.

- **Adaptation is Permanent:** Strategic HR is a permanent operating model that must continually measure and adapt its strategy to remain a relevant driver of enterprise value.[3]

Reflection

Use these questions to spark discussion with your leadership team.

- If a competitor hired away 10% of our top-performing Sales or Engineering team tomorrow, what would be the estimated financial impact on our P&L for the next two quarters?
- What is the single most compelling piece of data from our exit interviews that should force us to change our current management training priorities?
- Based on the recent market analysis, what is the next major technology or market condition that will render a significant portion of our current skills obsolete?
- How can we use the Quarterly Strategic Review to adjust the Executive Scorecard and ensure accountability for a recently identified talent risk?

Chapter 13: Scaling the Strategic Culture

Summary:

The ultimate measure of Strategic HR success is its ability to push talent accountability into the operational fabric of the company. Scaling the Strategic Culture involves converting all middle managers into active HR Partners by holding them accountable for strategic outcomes, ensuring the Employee Value Proposition (EVP) is authentically funded, and transforming administrative policies into codified rules that reinforce business agility.

Step-by-Step Framework

This chapter addresses the transition from a successfully implemented strategy (Chapters 1-12) to a permanently institutionalized operating model. The ultimate measure of Strategic HR success is its ability to push the principles and accountability for talent management down into the operational fabric of the company. This means the Strategic HR mindset must be adopted by every manager, and every administrative policy must reinforce the strategic direction. Scaling the Strategic Culture is the process of embedding talent accountability so deeply that the organization operates on a strategic HR system, ensuring the strategy endures beyond the initial implementation phase.

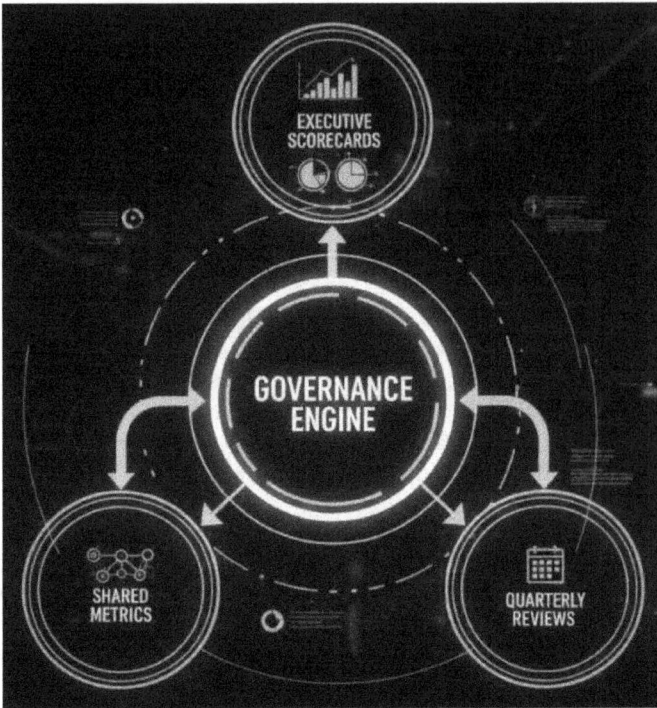

13.1 Manager as HR Partner: Pushing Accountability Down

Middle managers are not just recipients of policy; they are the primary, day-to-day executors of the talent strategy. If a manager focuses solely on clerical compliance (e.g., ticking boxes on forms), the entire strategic system will fail at the execution level, regardless of how brilliant the CEO-approved plan may be. Therefore, manager training must undergo a radical shift, moving away from basic legal compliance to focused instruction on leadership, coaching, and data-driven people decisions.

Crucially, this shift must be cemented by accountability. Managers must be formally held responsible through their own performance reviews for strategic outcomes, such as team engagement scores, internal promotion rates, Time-to-Productivity (TTTP) of new hires, and low regrettable turnover. This action converts managers from passive recipients of HR policy into active, accountable HR Partners in the talent strategy, ensuring consistency and buy-in across all operational units.

What It Is: Making middle managers directly accountable for strategic people outcomes through their performance reviews and focused training on data-driven people decisions, not just legal compliance.

Why It's Important for the Business: It ensures that the talent strategy is executed consistently across all departments and that management behavior supports, rather than sabotages, enterprise-wide goals such as retention and innovation. The manager becomes the chief owner of human capital risk for their team.

Blueprint for Institutionalizing Strategy: The Case Studies

The two case studies in this chapter are designed to demonstrate how to systemically embed talent accountability throughout the organization.

The first case study, Accountability Drives Retention (Finance), provides a non-negotiable template for converting a reluctant middle manager into an HR Partner. The purpose is to prove that the Manager Accountability model works. You should use the outcome to justify tying a percentage of manager bonuses directly to a strategic outcome (like team regrettable turnover), demonstrating that this structural change is the fastest way to drive cost reduction and solve execution-level problems.

The second case study, "Policy vs. Strategy (Media Startup)," focuses on the importance of governance structure. Its purpose is to show that a core administrative policy (the review and promotion process) can directly sabotage the entire strategic culture (innovation and autonomy). Use this example to audit your own policies, ensuring that every internal rule is intentionally designed to accelerate, not impede, your organization's core business mission and the promises of your EVP.

Case Study: Accountability Drives Retention (Finance)

Issue: A regional bank's call center division suffered from chronic, regrettable turnover (annually) despite offering high entry-level salaries. HR's data analysis revealed that the turnover was concentrated among managers.

Action Taken: (Manager Accountability): The HR Director implemented a two-part solution for the pilot group: 1) mandatory, data-driven manager training focused on team engagement strategies, and 2) a new policy making the manager's annual bonus dependent on keeping their team's regrettable turnover rate below the enterprise target.

Outcome: Within one year, the turnover rate for the accountable managers dropped too, saving the bank an estimated amount in replacement costs. The managers, incentivized to solve the problem, became active coaches rather than passive administrators, fundamentally solving the problem at the execution level where it originated.

13.2 The Employee Value Proposition (EVP): The Promise and the Proof

Discussion: The Employee Value Proposition (EVP) is the formal and informal promise the company makes to its current and future employees regarding what they will receive in exchange for their commitment (pay, benefits, development, career path, culture). The strategic initiatives you design (development plans, competitive pay bands, designed culture) are the physical manifestation of this promise. The EVP is, essentially, the marketing language for the strategic HR product. If the EVP promises "rapid growth and development," but the training budget is chronically small, promotions are rare, or the manager development system is nonexistent, the promise is fake. To attract and retain the critical talent identified in the Talent Forecast, the HR strategy must ensure the budget, policies, and practices authentically and consistently deliver on the EVP promise.

What It Is: The comprehensive promises a company makes to its employees; the strategic initiatives and allocated budget are the essential practices that fulfill this promise, ensuring the promise is credible.

Why It's Important for the Business: A credible EVP is essential for attracting and retaining the critical talent identified in the Talent Forecast (Chapter 3). When the promise is broken, turnover is inevitable, and recruitment costs skyrocket.

Actionable Steps: Auditing EVP Authenticity

- **Map the Promise:** Document the core pillars of the company's stated EVP (e.g., "Market-leading pay," "Innovation culture," "Rapid career growth").
- **Audit the Spend:** Directly compare the EVP pillars to the allocated budget (e.g., If the EVP is "Rapid career growth," but the development budget per employee is less than annually, the EVP is not authentically funded).

- **Validate the Policy:** Ensure core policies (e.g., compensation bands, promotion criteria) actively support the promise. If the EVP promises "meritocracy," the compensation policy must transparently reward high performance.

Formula in action – EVP Credibility Score

The EVP Credibility Score is a ratio demonstrating the financial commitment relative to the cost of failure (regrettable turnover).

EVP Credibility Score Completion

Metric	Placeholder	Value (Example)
Budget Allocated to Career Development: annually.	$B	$500,000

Metric	Placeholder	Value (Example)
Estimated Annual Cost of Regrettable Turnover for Young Talent (who value growth):	$T	**$2,000,000**

Calculation: EVP Credibility Score

The EVP Credibility Score is often calculated as the ratio of your investment in a specific EVP pillar to the financial cost of *failing* to deliver on that promise. A score greater than 1 suggests that your commitment is financially greater than the cost of failure, lending credibility to the promise.

Formula:

$$EVP\ Credibility\ Score = \frac{Budget\ Allocated\ to\ EVP\ Pillar}{Estimated\ Annual\ Cost\ of\ Regrettable\ Turnover\ Related\ to\ that\ Pillar}$$

Applying the Example:

$$EVP\ Credibility\ Score = \frac{\$500{,}000}{\$2{,}000{,}000}$$

$$EVP\ Credibility\ Score = 0.25$$

Interpretation

An EVP Credibility Score of 0.25 suggests that for every dollar lost due to regrettable turnover related to a lack of career growth, the company is only investing 25 cents into career development. This indicates a high risk that the "Rapid Career Growth" promise will be seen as fake, leading to continued regrettable turnover.

HR Maturity Progression Curve

Evolving from Administrative to Strategic Impact

Higher Organizational Value (y-axis)

Time / Value / Influence (x-axis)

Reactive HR
- Transactional Focus
- Compliance Driven

Proactive HR
- Process Improvement
- Program Implementation

Predictive HR
- Workforce Analytics
- Talent Forecasting

Strategic Partnership
- Business Integration
- Congment Value Creation

Increasing Strategic Impact

13.3 Governance and Policy: Codifying the Strategic Game

The final, structural step in scaling the culture is reviewing all administrative policies through a strategic lens. In a strategic culture, policies cease to be isolated administrative rules and become the codified rules of the strategic game. For example, if the strategy is "innovation and agility," then rigid, complex job classification policies that lock employees into narrow roles must be revised to allow for flexible job roles and cross-functional movement. Every policy must be intentionally designed to reinforce the desired culture and business strategy, ensuring the administrative structure does not inadvertently stifle the organization's ability to execute its core mission. This policy review is the ultimate act of ensuring the "plumbing" (Chapter 2) aligns with the "strategy" (Chapter 4).

What It Is: Reviewing and revising all administrative policies (e.g., compensation review schedules, promotion criteria, remote work guidelines) to ensure they actively support the desired culture and business strategy.

Why It's Important for the Business: It ensures the company's internal rules and governance structures enable, rather than restrict, the organization's ability to execute its core strategy (e.g., ensuring a flexible sick leave policy doesn't impede the culture of presenteeism necessary for high-trust collaboration).

Case Study: Policy vs. Strategy (Media Startup)

Issue: A fast-growing digital media startup promoted an EVP of "Innovation and High Autonomy." However, the -day performance review policy required managers to obtain three levels of mandatory approval before granting any promotion or significant raise. This bureaucratic policy directly contradicted the "rapid growth" EVP, causing high turnover among ambitious, high-performing new hires.

Action Taken (Policy Revision): HR used data (exit interviews citing "slow career progress") to prove the policy was the bottleneck. They revised the policy to grant managers the authority to approve raises and promotions up to a certain percentage threshold without the three-level review, provided the employee's performance data was clearly documented in the HRIS.

Outcome: The policy changes immediately accelerated promotion cycles for high performers by an average of 45 days. This alignment of policy with the EVP reduced regrettable turnover among high performers in the following quarter and reinforced the core cultural pillar of "High Autonomy."

Chapter 13 Checklist: Scaling the Strategic Culture

Action	Outcome
Action 1: Update manager performance reviews to include accountability for two strategic outcomes (e.g., team regrettable turnover, internal promotion rate).	Managers become active, accountable partners in the talent strategy.
Action 2: Conduct a review of core administrative policies (e.g., job	Policies support strategic goals rather

Action	Outcome
classification rules, compensation review processes) to ensure they reinforce the desired culture/strategy.	than creating bureaucracy.
Action 3: Audit whether the **Employee Value Proposition (EVP)** aligns with the actual budget allocated for training and development, and adjust either the budget or the promise.	Ensures the company's talent promises are credible and defensible.

Key Takeaways

- **Accountability is Execution:** Convert managers into HR Partners by tying their performance reviews and bonuses directly to strategic talent outcomes like retention and internal mobility.
- **EVP Authenticity:** The Employee Value Proposition must be authentically backed by the budget and policies; a fake promise is a guarantee of high turnover.
- **Codify the Culture:** Review and revise all administrative policies to ensure they act as codified rules of the strategic game, enabling agility and innovation, not inhibiting them.
- **Systemic Scaling:** The goal is to embed the strategic HR function so deeply that the organization runs on the strategic talent system, ensuring the strategy's permanence.

Reflection

Use these questions to spark discussion with your leadership team.

- If we audited manager bonuses, what percentage of the reward is tied to financial or operational execution versus strategic talent outcomes?
- Which specific element of our current Employee Value Proposition (EVP) is most likely to be exposed as a "fake promise" due to insufficient budget or restrictive policy?

- If our business strategy is "rapid innovation," which existing HR or administrative policy is currently the biggest bottleneck to cross-functional movement and job role flexibility?
- How can we redesign a core manager training program to focus on coaching and data analysis, and only on legal compliance?

STRATEGIC MATURITY CHECKLIST

- ☑ Governance
- ☑ Data
- ☑ Collaboration
- ☑ Adaptability
- ☑ Financial Literacy

Chapter 14: The Ultimate Competitive Advantage

Summary

The journey from administrative function to Strategic HR is complete when the function is viewed as the essential core of the business itself. The challenges of the modern economy are fundamentally people problems, and the strategic HR function, through its use of data and foresight, is the only one equipped to provide the organization with its ultimate, sustainable competitive advantage.

Step-by-Step Framework

The transition described throughout these chapters, from transactional processor to strategic partner, reaches its final stage when the executive suite universally views the HR function not as a service provider to the business, but as the essential core of the business itself. This concept, often summarized as HR is the Business, signifies that human capital strategy is no longer a supporting function but the primary lever for competitive advantage, market adaptation, and risk mitigation.

The challenges of the modern economy, including the rapid integration of Artificial Intelligence (AI) into workflows, the accelerating pace of skill obsolescence, and the inherent complexity of managing highly distributed global workforces, are all fundamentally people problems. A tactical HR function, one focused merely on compliance and maintenance, will inevitably collapse under the weight of these seismic, talent-driven changes. The strategic HR function, with its demonstrated capability in Talent Forecasting, Risk Mitigation, and Data Storytelling, is the only one equipped to ensure the organization not only survives but sustainably thrives in this volatile environment. By mastering the frameworks presented, the HR leader has established the firm's most resilient and proprietary competitive edge: a highly effective system for managing its most valuable asset.

14.1 Blueprint for Final Action: The Launch Sequence and the Ultimate Payoff

The conclusion contains two crucial elements: the 90-Day Launch Sequence and the Proven Result callout. The purpose of the 90-Day Launch Sequence is to provide a final, actionable roadmap that integrates the best practices from every preceding chapter, from capacity creation (Month 1) to partnership building (Month 3), into a single, executable plan. Use this sequence as a checklist for your first three months in the strategic role, ensuring an immediate, high-impact focus. The Proven Result callout, Translating HR Strategy to Valuation, is the ultimate payoff example. Its purpose is to demonstrate that the journey doesn't just reduce cost; it adds millions to the company's market valuation by proving organizational maturity and mitigating investor risk. You should use this outcome to communicate the final, highest-level financial justification for the entire Strategic HR function to the CEO and the Board.

Proven Result – Translating HR Strategy to Valuation

The 90-Day Launch Sequence: Your Actionable Roadmap

The 90-Day Launch Sequence provides a final, actionable roadmap to integrate all best practices into a single, high-impact plan.

- **Purpose:** To guide your first three months in the strategic HR role. It serves as a comprehensive checklist for immediate execution.

- **Structure:** The sequence moves from foundational steps like capacity creation (Month 1) to critical activities such as partnership building (Month 3), ensuring an immediate, focused, and high-impact start.

The Ultimate Payoff: Translating HR Strategy to Valuation

The Proven Result callout is the ultimate financial example demonstrating that your strategic HR journey doesn't just reduce operational cost; it actively adds millions to the company's market valuation. Use this outcome to communicate the final, highest-level financial justification for the entire Strategic HR function to the CEO and the Board.

Case Study: HR Strategy Drives Valuation Uplift

A private manufacturing firm successfully completed the Strategic HR transition phase, resulting in a demonstrable financial impact during a capital raise.

- **Key HR Metrics Presented to Investors:**

    - **Succession Readiness Score:** Improved from 45% to 85% (demonstrating mitigation of leadership risk).

    - **Annualized Cost of Regrettable Turnover:** Reduced by $1.5 Million (demonstrating efficiency and retention of high-value talent).

- **Investor Impact:** A major private equity (P.E.) group assessed the firm's valuation. They explicitly cited the documented HR risk management (the high Succession Readiness Score) and demonstrated efficiency metrics as proof of Organizational Maturity.

- **Financial Outcome:** Due to this proven stability and predictability, which fundamentally mitigates execution risk, the P.E. group approved the capital raise at a valuation multiple 0.5 points higher than the initial average. This resulted in an additional $25 million in valuation. Strategic HR was cited as the key factor protecting the future cash flow required to justify the higher multiple.

14.2 The Perpetual Strategic Mandate

The completion of the final phase simply marks the beginning of the continuous, permanent strategic operating model. The Strategic HR leader's mandate is perpetual, requiring constant monitoring and adaptation. The established governance mechanisms (Quarterly Strategic Reviews, Executive

Scorecards, Shared Metrics) are the engine of this permanence, ensuring the function can adapt to inevitable changes:

- **Talent Risk:** The continuous need to model Succession Readiness Scores and quantify the Cost of Regrettable Turnover remains crucial as key leaders and specialized skill holders move between companies.

- **Adaptability:** The Talent Forecast is now a living document, constantly updated to reflect technology adoption (e.g., modeling the skills needed for the next generation of AI tools) and geopolitical market expansion (e.g., forecasting the need for regulatory experts in a new region).

- **Financial Value:** Every proposal must continue to use the Finance Filter to justify its existence, proving that every dollar spent on a person is an investment in revenue, cost reduction, or risk mitigation.

90-DAY HR STRATEGIC LAUNCH SEQUENCE

Accelerating New Initiatives for Impact

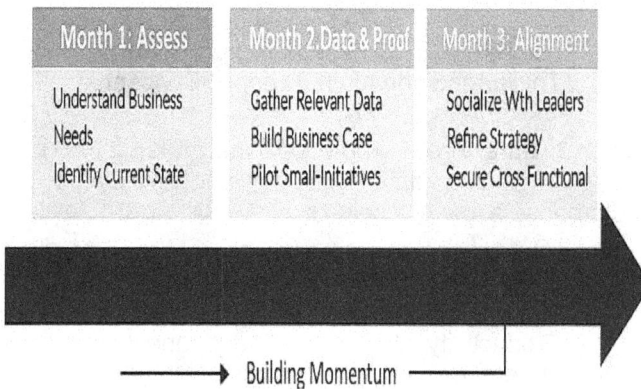

Month 1: Assess	Month 2. Data & Proof	Month 3: Alignment
Understand Business Needs	Gather Relevant Data	Socialize Wth Leaders
Identify Current State	Build Business Case	Refine Strategy
	Pilot Small-Initiatives	Secure Cross Functional

Building Momentum

14.3 Your Next 90 Days: The Launch Sequence

The transition from tactical to strategic requires a focused, disciplined launch sequence. The following 90-Day Plan integrates the essential actions from the preceding chapters into a phased, high-impact schedule designed to build capacity, gather data, and secure executive buy-in immediately.

Month 1: Assess and Free Capacity (Phase 1 Focus) The goal is to eliminate the administrative burden, creating capacity and establishing the initial data baseline.

- **Conduct the HR Audit and Process-Time-Cost Analysis:** Meticulously map the top administrative time sinks. Calculate the annual dollar cost of the sunk administrative labor to establish the financial justification for automation.

- **Automate the Quick Win:** Secure approval (leveraging the quantified cost) to automate the single most time-consuming administrative task (e.g., time-off requests, compliance filing). This immediately frees up capacity and demonstrates HR's commitment to efficiency.

- **Anchor the Strategy:** Schedule a dedicated one-on-one meeting with the CEO or President to identify and confirm their single biggest operational "people pain point" (e.g., high defects in production, slow sales cycle). This targets the future Proof-of-Concept.

Month 2: Data, Proof, and Proposal (Phase 2 Focus) The goal is to leverage clean data to quantify a costly business problem and propose a low-risk solution.

- **Calculate Strategic Baselines:** Calculate the current annual Cost of Regrettable Turnover and the Time-to-Productivity (TTTP) baseline for one critical, revenue-generating role. This establishes the two core financial metrics for the PoC.

- **Design the PoC:** Design a small, low-cost Proof-of-Concept (PoC) intervention (e.g., a day manager coaching program) specifically to address the CEO's pain point identified in Month 1.

- **Draft the Financial Proposal:** Draft a one-page, financially focused proposal for the PoC. Ensure the proposal leads with the ROI using the Finance Filter, stating the quantifiable risk that the small investment will mitigate. Use a Three-Slide Deck format for rehearsal.

Sample Proposal Deck:

Here is a narrative outline for the 3-slide executive proposal deck, designed to be rehearsed and delivered in under five minutes.

The 3-Slide "Proof-of-Concept" Proposal

This deck is designed to follow the "Finance Filter." It's a financial proposal, not an HR presentation. The narrative moves from a massive, quantified problem to a low-risk, high-return "ask."

Slide 1: The Problem & Its Price Tag

Goal: To shock the executive audience by attaching a precise, multi-million-dollar cost to a business problem they already *feel* anecdotally. You are establishing the financial baseline for *inaction*.

Slide Title: The Hidden $4.2M Drain on Our Revenue *(Note: Use a specific, calculated number in the title).*

Narrative Flow:

1. **Acknowledge the Pain Point (The CEO's Words):** "In our last meeting, you (the CEO) noted that we're 'failing to keep our best sales talent.' You were right. We've run the numbers, and the problem is more significant than we imagined."

2. **Quantify the Pain (The Strategic Baselines):**

   o "First, we're losing our best people. Our Annualized Cost of Regrettable Turnover for our top 20% of Sales Directors is $2.7 Million." (This is the *cost of failure*).

   o "Second, it's taking us too long to recover. Our Time-to-Productivity for a new Sales Director is 8.5 Months. That's over $1.5M in lost revenue potential and ramp-up costs *per role*."

3. **The "Cliffhanger" (Transition to Slide 2):** "This is a $4.2 million problem. But the data shows it's not a compensation problem. It's a coaching problem. And we believe it's fixable with a small, surgical test."

Slide 2: The Low-Risk Solution (The PoC)**

Goal: To introduce a small-scale, low-cost "Proof-of-Concept" (PoC) that directly addresses the root cause from Slide 1. This de-risks the "yes" for the executive.

Slide Title: A Proposed Solution: The 30-Day 'Manager-as-Coach' PoC

Flow:

1. **Introduce the PoC:** "We are not proposing a massive, company-wide training. We are proposing a 30-day Proof-of-Concept focused *only* on the 12 managers in our highest-turnover sales division."

2. **Define the Intervention (The "How"):** "The PoC is a lightweight, one-day manager coaching program. It's not about theory; it's about giving them the tools to have *one* effective career conversation and *one* weekly performance check-in."

3. **Define Success:** "This is a test. We are not asking for a full rollout. We are asking to *prove* that this low-cost intervention can move our multi-million-dollar turnover

metric. We will measure success by a 50% reduction in regrettable turnover *within this group* over the next 6 months."

Slide 3: The Financial Proposal & The ROI

Goal: To frame the "ask" as a clear, high-return investment, not a cost. This is the "Finance Filter" in action.

Slide Title: The Financial Case: A 20x Potential Return

Flow:

1. **State the ROI First:** "This proposal isn't a cost; it's an investment. The projected return is 20-to-1. We are asking to invest $75,000 to mitigate a $1.5 million portion of our annual turnover cost."

2. **The "Ask" (The Investment):**

   o **What:** "A one-time cost of **$75,000**." (This covers the coaching program development and tools for the PoC).

   o **When:** "We can launch this in 10 days."

3. **The Payoff (The Return):**

   o **PoC GOAL:** Reduce regrettable turnover in the PoC group by 50%.

   o **FINANCIAL IMPACT:** This single PoC will mitigate an annualized $1.5 Million in turnover costs.

   o **THE BOTTOM LINE:** "This is a low-risk, high-return experiment to prove we can solve our talent problem. We are asking for your approval on this $75,000 investment to protect $1.5 million in value."

Month 3: Alignment and Partnership (Phase 3 Focus) The goal is to secure funding, build collaboration with peers, and institutionalize the strategic mindset within the HR team.

- **Secure PoC Approval:** Present the PoC proposal to the executive team using the financial filter and the Data Storytelling framework. Secure a small budget commitment.

- **Initiate Partnership:** Initiate a "Shared Metrics" conversation (Chapter 9) with one key peer leader (e.g., VP of Operations, CFO). Propose joint accountability for a specific business outcome directly related to the PoC (e.g., jointly owning the "Cost of Quality" metric).

- **Develop the Team:** Begin cross-training your HR staff on basic business finance and metrics, focusing on reading the company's P&L statement. Update job descriptions for all open roles that require business acumen.

Strategic HR Engine
Powering Business Success Through People

Key Takeaways

- **HR is the Business:** The strategic HR function is the essential core of the modern organization, providing the only viable competitive advantage against talent-driven market volatility.

- **90-Day Discipline:** The transition requires a disciplined, three-month launch sequence focused on creating capacity, quantifying cost, and securing PoC funding.

- **Sustained Credibility:** Strategic influence is maintained through perpetual accountability via the Quarterly Strategic Review and the active management of organizational risk.

- **The Power of People:** The ability to proactively manage human capital—to forecast, develop, and retain the right skills—is the ultimate differentiator and the true power available to the Strategic HR leader.

Reflection

Use these questions to spark discussion with your leadership team.

- If a major competitor were to adopt our strategic HR operating model tomorrow, what is the single biggest advantage they would gain over us?

- Which one of the Executive Scorecard metrics (Succession Readiness, Turnover Cost, or Skills Gap) currently poses the greatest unmitigated risk to our year-long strategic plan?

- Based on our current organizational structure, is there a single executive whose failure to collaborate could still derail the entire people strategy?

- If we audited the time spent by all executives on talent issues, what percentage of that time is spent on reactive problem-solving versus proactive strategy and forecasting?

Strategic HR Tools and Supporting Chapters

Tool/Model/Framework	Description & Strategic Application	Primary Chapters Supported
Process-Time-Cost Analysis	A metric that translates wasted time on manual, administrative tasks (sunk administrative labor) into a quantifiable dollar cost. It is the core financial justification for automation investment	1, 2, 14 (Month 1)
Finance Filter	The mandatory communication framework requires every HR proposal to justify its existence based on its measurable effect on one of three financial levers: Increase Revenue, Decrease Cost, or Mitigate Risk	1, 5, 6, 14
Cost of Regrettable Turnover Formula	A metric used to quantify the financial risk of talent loss, typically approximated as the Departing Employee's Salary times 1.5. It forces management to focus on avoiding this cost.	1, 3, 7, 12, 14 (Month 2)
Time-to-Productivity (TTTP) Metric	Measures the time (in weeks or months) from a new employee's start date until they are performing at 90% or more of expected efficiency. It links HR	3, 6, 12, 14 (Month 2)

Tool/Model/Framework	Description & Strategic Application	Primary Chapters Supported
	efficiency directly to revenue acceleration or project speed	
Talent Forecast (Gap Analysis)	The ultimate predictive function of Strategic HR. It compares future skill requirements (Demand) with the current workforce skills (Supply) to identify the critical gap.	1, 3, 4, 12
Succession Readiness Score	A quantifiable metric that reports the company's vulnerability to losing critical leaders (Talent Risk) by assessing the internal pipeline for key roles (Score 0-3).	4, 7, 12
Buy, Build, or Borrow Framework	The strategic decision matrix for closing skill gaps identified in the Talent Forecast balances speed, cost, and risk in sourcing talent.	4
Shared Metrics	Key Performance Indicators (KPIs) tracked and owned jointly by HR and one or more peer leaders (e.g., HR/Operations on Cost of Quality). This enforces collaboration by making failure a shared financial burden.	8, 9, 10, 14

Tool/Model/Framework	Description & Strategic Application	Primary Chapters Supported
Proof-of-Concept (PoC) Strategy	A small, contained, high-visibility pilot project designed to generate rapid, quantifiable financial results (ROI) within a short period (90 days). It mitigates executive risk and secures buy-in.	6, 14 (Month 2, 3)
Executive Scorecard	The formal, top-level performance reporting used by the CEO and Board. Strategic HR advocates for including key talent metrics (e.g., Succession Readiness Score) to institutionalize accountability.	7, 12, 14
Process Standardization ("One Best Way")	Establishing the ideal, standard workflow for core HR processes (e.g., Candidate Interview Loop) to ensure data is consistent, comparable, and reliable for strategic analysis.	2, 8
HRIS/HCM Platform	The technological backbone (viewed as Critical Data Infrastructure) that enforces Employee Self-Service (ESS) to automate administrative work and enforces clean data integration.	2

90-Day Rollout Plan: Transitioning HR from Tactical to Strategic

Purpose

To reposition the HR function as a strategic partner aligned with organizational goals, moving from reactive administration to proactive business leadership.

Phase 1: Foundation & Assessment (Days 1–30)

Objective: Understand the current state of HR, establish credibility, and define strategic priorities.

Key Actions

1. **Executive Alignment**

   - Meet with the CEO and key leaders to clarify business goals, financial targets, and workforce challenges.

   - Identify 3–5 critical business outcomes HR must directly support (e.g., productivity, retention, talent readiness).

2. **HR Capability & Process Audit**

   - Evaluate all current HR processes (recruiting, onboarding, performance, compensation, compliance, etc.) for efficiency, business impact, and technology use.

   - Categorize activities such as *Strategic*, *Operational*, or *Administrative*.

3. **Data & Metrics Baseline**
   - Establish baseline measures for turnover, time-to-fill, cost-per-hire, engagement, absenteeism, and revenue per employee.
   - Audit HR systems and data quality.

4. **Stakeholder Feedback**

   o Conduct leadership interviews or surveys to assess HR's current reputation and service effectiveness.

   o Document perceived strengths, weaknesses, and expectations.

5. **Quick Wins**

   o Identify two or three visible improvements (e.g., faster hiring workflow, onboarding checklist, HR response standards) to build confidence.

Deliverables

- HR Diagnostic Report (current vs. desired state)

- Initial KPI dashboard

- Executive summary of priorities and gaps

Phase 2: Strategic Design & Capability Building (Days 31–60)

Objective: Design the future HR model and build capabilities for strategic delivery.

Key Actions

1. **Define the Strategic HR Vision**

   o Create an HR mission statement aligned to business goals.

   o Clarify HR's value proposition: *"HR as a profit-enabling function."*

2. **Develop HR Strategy and Roadmap**

   o Map 3–5 strategic priorities (e.g., workforce planning, leadership development, culture & engagement, analytics).

   o Establish objectives, metrics, and ownership for each.

3. **Restructure HR Work**

   o Reallocate time and resources from administrative tasks to strategic activities.

   o Delegate transactional work to automation, shared services, or external partners.

4. **Build Leadership & Analytical Skills**

   o Train HR team in business acumen, financial literacy, and data-driven decision-making.

   o Introduce analytics tools or dashboards to demonstrate ROI.

5. **Communicate the Plan**

   o Present the new HR strategy and roadmap to the executive team.

   o Share early progress and metrics through visual scorecards.

Deliverables

- HR Strategic Framework and 12-month roadmap

- Updated HR structure and role alignment

- Skill-building and analytics training plan

Phase 3: Implementation & Integration (Days 61–90)

Objective: Execute early strategic initiatives and embed HR into business planning.

Key Actions

1. **Launch Strategic Initiatives**

   o   Begin pilot projects in 1–2 critical areas (e.g., workforce planning, leadership development, or retention strategy).

   o   Use measurable outcomes to show business impact.

2. **Integrate HR into Business Operations**

   o   Participate in regular business reviews and operational planning meetings.

   o   Align HR metrics with company scorecards (e.g., turnover cost reduction, productivity gains).

3. **Refine Policies and Technology**

   o   Modernize policies and systems to support agile HR operations.

   o   Introduce data dashboards for real-time reporting.

4. **Communicate Wins & Reinforce Culture Change**

   o   Report early results to executives and employees.

   o   Share success stories demonstrating HR's new strategic role.

5. **Prepare for Long-Term Continuity**

   o Draft a 6-month continuation plan for sustaining strategic HR practices.

   o Establish governance for continuous improvement and quarterly reviews.

Deliverables

- Strategic HR Pilot Report (results, metrics, feedback)

- Updated dashboards and communication materials

- 6-Month Strategic HR Continuity Plan

Summary of Milestones

Timeline	Focus	Key Deliverables
Days 1–30	Assess & Align	HR diagnostic, KPI baseline, executive alignment
Days 31–60	Design & Build	HR strategy, roadmap, capability development
Days 61–90	Implement & Integrate	Pilot outcomes, dashboards, continuity plan

Core Strategic HR Formulas for SMBs

Formula/Metric	Purpose & Supporting Chapters	Example
1. Cost of Sunk Administrative Labor	**Phase 1: Quantifying Inefficiency (Chapter 2, 1).** Measures the recurring salary expense paid for non-value-added manual work (the Tactical Trap). This is the core evidence to justify investment in automation.	Cost = Fully Loaded Hourly Rate times Total Annual Hours Spent on Manual Task
2. Cost of Regrettable Turnover (Replacement Cost)	**Quantifying Financial Risk (Chapter 1, 3, 7).** This formula quantifies the total financial expense incurred when an employee leaves and must be replaced, justifying investment in retention programs. It uses the conservative 1.5 salary multiplier, as often cited in business literature.	Cost of Regrettable Turnover = approx. departing Employee's Fully Loaded Annual Salary times 1.5
3. Lost Revenue/Increased Cost of Production	**Linking Quality to Cost (Chapter 5, 7).** This formula quantifies the financial impact of a process failure or a drop in quality, linking the HR action (e.g., lack of training or high turnover) directly to the Cost of Goods Sold (COGS) or operational expenses.	lost Revenue/Increased Cost = Unit Cost of Failure $\times$ Number of Defective units/Incidents + Cost of Rework/Warranty
4. Delayed Revenue Contribution (TTTP Cost)	**Measuring Onboarding Efficiency (Chapter 3, 6).** This formula quantifies the	Delayed Revenue Contribution Cost = Role's Annual Revenue Contribution

Formula/Metric	Purpose & Supporting Chapters	Example
	cost of the time delay between a new employee starting and becoming fully proficient, linking the efficiency of HR's recruiting and onboarding process to the company's revenue acceleration.	52 Weeks) times Time-to-Productivity in Weeks
5. Return on Investment (ROI)	**Justifying Strategic Investment (Chapter 5, 6)**. Proves to the executive team that an HR initiative is not a cost, but a profitable investment by translating program cost into financial benefit.	ROI = Financial Benefit - Cost of Investment / Cost of Investment times 100
6. Fully Loaded Salary Cost	**Quantifying Administrative Burden (Chapter 1)**. Used as the basis for calculating both Sunk Administrative Labor and Turnover Cost. It accurately reflects the *true* organizational cost of an employee.	Fully Loaded Salary = Base Salary times 1 + Benefits Load
7. Succession Readiness Score (Percentage)	**Quantifying Leadership Risk (Chapter 4, 7)**. A quantifiable metric reported to the C-Suite to assess the company's vulnerability to losing critical leaders (Talent Risk).	The maximum possible score is calculated by multiplying the number of roles by the maximum score per role. The readiness score percentage Is found by dividing the sum of the critical role readiness scores by

Formula/Metric	Purpose & Supporting Chapters	Example
		the maximum possible score and then multiplying the result by 100.
8. Revenue Per Employee	**Measuring Workforce Efficiency (Chapter 3)**. The simplest measure used to link talent quality and strategic HR initiatives (e.g., training) to overall organizational profitability and efficiency.	Revenue Per Employee = Total Revenue / Total Number of Employees
9. Talent Gap Analysis	**Predictive Workforce Planning (Chapter 1, 3)**. A simple equation used to proactively identify future skill deficits and inform the "Buy" or "Build" talent strategy, ensuring the company has the necessary capacity for future growth.	Critical Gap = Future Demand - Current Supply
10. EVP Credibility Score	**Authenticating the Talent Promise (Chapter 13)**. Quantifies the risk that the company's talent promises (Employee Value Proposition - EVP) are seen as fake due to insufficient funding, which can lead to regrettable turnover.	EVP Credibility Score = Budget Allocated to Development / Cost of Regrettable Turnover for Target Talent

Key Strategic HR Frameworks and Tools

The following five tools are the essential operational and strategic disciplines required to transform the Human Resources function from administrative overhead into a Strategic Business Partner. They are critical because they force HR to shift from subjective, reactive management to objective, measurable, and predictive planning. While the Eisenhower Matrix is a time management tool that helps HR leaders escape the administrative "Tactical Trap," the others are frameworks that directly translate HR activities into financial and strategic results, which is the only language the C-Suite understands.

1. 9-Box Grid

The **9-Box Grid** is a popular talent management tool used to assess, plot, and visualize an organization's **talent pool** based on two primary factors: Performance and Potential.

Purpose and Use

- **Purpose:** To help leadership identify high-potential employees (HiPOs) for succession planning, target specific development needs, and make objective decisions about resource allocation for talent (e.g., who to invest in versus who to manage out).

- **Strategic Outcome:** Provides a quick, consensus-based visual map of the entire workforce, preventing subjective decision-making in promotions and development.

- **Best Used For:** Succession planning, development program allocation, and workforce planning reviews.

How to Use the 9-Box Grid

1. **Define Axes:** Clearly define the criteria for the three levels of Current Performance (Y-axis: Low, Medium, High) and the three levels of Future Potential (X-axis: Low, Medium, High).

2. **Gather Data:** Collect objective data points (e.g., performance review scores, project results, 360-degree feedback) to assess the Performance axis. Assess Potential based on competencies such as learning agility, ambition, and critical thinking.

3. **Plot Employees:** Plot each employee into one of the nine boxes based on their combined scores.

4. **Action Strategy:** Apply the standard action strategy for each box (e.g., "High Performance/High Potential" = Maximize/Invest Heavily; "Low Performance/Low Potential" = Manage Out/Reassign).

9-Box Grid Template

	Future Potential: Low	Future Potential: Medium	Future Potential: High
Current Performance: High	2. **Consistent Contributor** (Reward, Retain, No Promotion Track)	5. **Key Contributor** (Develop & Retain, Monitor Potential)	8. **Star/High Potential** (Accelerate, Maximize Investment)
Current Performance: Medium	1. **Effective** (Review for Fit, Monitor)	4. **Core Employee** (Maintain, Standard Development)	7. **High Impact** (Coach, Promote within 12-18 months)
Current Performance: Low	0. **Risk/Manage Out** (Improve or Exit, No Investment)	3. **Inconsistent** (Address Performance, Potential Unclear)	6. **Questionable** (Address Performance, High-Risk Investment)

2. Balanced Scorecard (BSC)

The Balanced Scorecard is a strategic framework used to translate an organization's mission and strategy into a comprehensive set of performance measures. It moves beyond purely financial metrics to include three other critical organizational perspectives.

Purpose and Use

- **Purpose:** To provide a "balanced" view of organizational performance by connecting strategy (mission/vision) to measurable operational activities and ensuring non-financial drivers of future performance (like learning and customers) are actively managed.

- **Strategic Outcome:** Clarifies the strategy and helps communicate what needs to be done to drive success across all functions, ensuring every HR metric (Chapter 3) is linked to a higher business outcome.

- **Best Used For:** Strategy formulation, executive performance reporting, and alignment across departments.

How to Use the Balanced Scorecard

1. **Define Strategy:** Start with the organization's strategic objectives (e.g., "Be the market leader in product quality").

2. **Establish Perspectives:** Structure the objectives across the four standard perspectives, asking the linking questions for each:

    o **Financial:** To succeed financially, how should we appear to our shareholders? (e.g., Increase ROI.)

    o **Customer:** To achieve our vision, how should we look to our customers? (e.g., Improve Customer Satisfaction.)

- o **Internal Process:** To satisfy our shareholders and customers, at what processes must we excel? (e.g., Reduce defect rate.)

- o **Learning & Growth (HR):** To achieve our vision, how will we sustain our ability to change and improve? (e.g., Improve employee skills and retention.)

3. **Define Metrics:** Define 2-3 measurable KPIs for each perspective and assign a target goal.

Balanced Scorecard Template

Perspective	Objective	Key Performance Indicator (KPI)	Target Goal	Initiatives	
Financial	Increase shareholder value	Revenue Per Employee		$350,000	Cost reduction via automation
Customer	Become preferred vendor	Customer Satisfaction (Net Promoter Score)		+60	Customer service training
Internal Process	Improve operational efficiency	Defect Rate (Units per 10,000		<50}	Standardized production workflow (HR: training rigor)
Learning & Growth (HR)	Ensure talent readiness	Succession Readiness Score		85%	Leadership development program

3. ADKAR Model

ADKAR is a change management model that focuses on the people side of change. It provides a structured sequence for ensuring that an individual successfully adopts a new process, system, or organizational structure. 47 It is essential for managing the organizational shifts required by Strategic HR (Chapter 11, Change Management Consultant).

Purpose and Use

- **Purpose:** To guide individuals through change by identifying the specific stages they must progress through and pinpointing where resistance or failure occurs. It ensures the change isn't just implemented but is truly adopted.

- **Strategic Outcome:** Increases the speed and success rate of strategic HR rollouts (e.g., implementing a new performance management system or HCM platform) by proactively addressing employee/manager concerns.

- **Best Used For:** Planning and diagnosing resistance to change initiatives.

How to Use the ADKAR Model

The model is a sequential, mandatory journey:

1. **Awareness (A):** The individual must understand why the change is needed. (Communicate the financial pain point.)

2. **Desire (D):** The individual must choose to support the change. (Communicate the personal benefit/consequence of not changing.)

3. **Knowledge (K):** The individual must know how to change. (Provide training and instruction.)

4. **Ability (A):** The individual must be able to perform the new skills. (Provide coaching and practice.)

5. **Reinforcement (R):** The change must stick. (Provide recognition, rewards, and audit results.)

ADKAR Diagnostic Template

ADKAR Element	Description / Result	Diagnostic Question (For Manager)	Action to Implement/Remedy
Awareness	Understand the financial reason for the change.	Do my team members understand the financial cost of our current method?	Executive presentation on the ROI/Risk Mitigation.
Desire	Willingness to participate and support.	Is my team actively sabotaging or passively resisting the new process?	Incentivize compliance (e.g., tie a bonus to a new metric).
Knowledge	Knows what to do.	Does my team know the steps of the new Candidate Interview Loop?	Formal training and documented procedures.
Ability	Can actually execute the change.	Can my team execute the new process	Practice, hands-on workshops, and 1:1 coaching.

ADKAR Element	Description / Result	Diagnostic Question (For Manager)	Action to Implement/Remedy
		efficiently and without coaching?	
Reinforcement	Change is sustained and rewarded.	Are we rewarding the old behavior or the new strategic behavior?	Audit data, celebrate early adopters, link new metric to P&L.

4. Kirkpatrick Model (Four Levels of Training Evaluation)

The Kirkpatrick Model is the standard framework for evaluating the effectiveness of training and development programs. Strategic HR utilizes it to move beyond simple attendance records and demonstrates that training has a financial impact (Chapter 3).

Purpose and Use

- **Purpose:** To provide a four-level hierarchy for measuring training outcomes, ensuring evaluation progresses from basic satisfaction to hard, measurable business results.

- **Strategic Outcome:** Proves the ROI of training investments (Chapter 5) by linking development programs to tangible business metrics like sales, safety incidents, or defect rates.

- **Best Used For:** Designing training evaluation metrics and proving the financial worth of development budgets.

How to Use the Kirkpatrick Model

Measurement must occur sequentially at all four levels 79:

1. **Reaction (Level 1):** Measures how participants feel about the training (satisfaction). (e.g., Post-course survey.)

2. **Learning (Level 2):** Measures what knowledge or skills participants gained. (e.g., Test scores, certification completion.)

3. **Behavior (Level 3):** Measures if participants applied the learning back on the job. (e.g., Manager observation, 360-degree feedback, audit scores.)

4. **Results (Level 4):** Measures the impact on the organization's bottom line. (e.g., reduced turnover,

increased sales, lower accident rate. This is the Financial Result.)

Kirkpatrick Model Evaluation Template

Level	Focus of Measurement	Example Metric for Manager Training	HR Strategic Value	
1. Reaction	Participant satisfaction		4.5/5 score on post-course survey	**Administrative**: Did they hate it?
2. Learning	Knowledge / Skill gain		90% pass rate on final coaching skills quiz	**Tactical**: Do they know the theory?
3. Behavior	Application on the job		75% of managers now conduct weekly 1:1 coaching sessions (audited)	**Tactical**: Are they actually doing the new behavior?
4. Results	Business Outcome/ROI		20% reduction in the team's regrettable turnover rate	**Strategic**: Did the training generate a financial return?

5. Eisenhower Matrix (Urgent/Important)

The Eisenhower Matrix is a time management and prioritization tool used to strategically categorize tasks and decisions based on their Urgency and Importance. It is the essential tool for escaping the Tactical Trap (Chapter 1) by forcing HR professionals to dedicate their capacity to strategic, high-impact work.

Purpose and Use

- **Purpose:** To provide a filter for daily tasks, forcing the HR leader to spend less time on urgent, low-importance administrative work (the Tactical Trap) and more time on high-importance, high-impact strategic work.

- **Strategic Outcome:** Ensures the newly freed capacity (Chapter 2) is used for strategic initiatives rather than reactive "firefighting".

- **Best Used For:** Daily task prioritization, delegation, and managing workload to maximize strategic time.

How to Use the Eisenhower Matrix

Categorize every task into one of the four quadrants and take the corresponding action:

1. **Urgent & Important (Quadrant 1): Do** immediately (Crises, deadlines).

2. **Not Urgent & Important (Quadrant 2): Plan** (Strategic planning, relationship building, development). This is the Strategic HR Quadrant.

3. **Urgent & Not Important (Quadrant 3):** Delegate (Interruptions, routine administrative tasks, low-value email). This is the Tactical Trap.

4. **Not Urgent & Not Important (Quadrant 4):** Eliminate (Time-wasting activities, busy work).

Eisenhower Matrix Template

This prioritization tool forces HR leaders to strategically categorize tasks to escape the Tactical Trap and dedicate time to high-impact strategic work.

Quadrant	Urgency	Importance	Action	HR Example
1. DO	High	High	Immediate action	Major compliance audit deadline, critical leader resigns.
2. PLAN (Strategic)	Low	High	Schedule, focus, dedicate time	Talent forecasting, Alignment Workshop preparation, Competency Model design.
3. DELEGATE	High	Low	Hand off/Automate	Manual payroll data entry, managing basic employee time-off requests, and routine compliance filing.
4. ELIMINATE	Low	Low	Don't do	Non-essential internal emails, low-value meetings, and

Quadrant	Urgency	Importance	Action	HR Example
				disorganized paper filing.

Strategic Business Glossary

Strategic Acronyms and Financial Terms

Term	Definition	Context in Strategic Terms (Simplified)
AI (Artificial Intelligence)	Computer systems that simulate human thinking for learning and problem-solving.	Plan for which jobs may be replaced by AI and retrain employees for future roles.
APAC (Asia-Pacific)	A region including Asia and the countries around the Pacific Ocean.	Used when planning business growth or market expansion.
ATS (Applicant Tracking System)	Software used to manage job applications and candidate data.	Provides data for workforce and hiring forecasts.
The company (Capital Expenditure)	Money is spent to buy or upgrade buildings, equipment, or other physical assets.	Reminds leaders to invest in both people and physical assets.

Term	Definition	Context in Strategic Terms (Simplified)
CEO (Chief Executive Officer)	The top executive responsible for overall company direction and performance.	The main audience for HR and business strategy reports.
CFO (Chief Financial Officer)	The executive responsible for financial planning, reporting, and budgeting.	A key partner who expects HR to use financial language and logic.
CHRO (Chief Human Resources Officer)	The top HR leader responsible for the entire people strategy.	Leads the organization's HR transformation and alignment.
COO (Chief Operating Officer)	The executive oversees daily operations and business processes.	A critical partner for improving efficiency and stability.
C-Suite	The group of senior executives, such as the CEO, CFO, COO, and CHRO.	The decision-making group that approves strategy and budgets.
CX (Customer Experience)	The total experience a customer has when interacting with a company.	HR helps improve CX by training employees to deliver better service.

Term	Definition	Context in Strategic Terms (Simplified)
EBITDA (Earnings Before Interest, Taxes, Depreciation, and Amortization)	A key measure of operating profit and business performance.	HR metrics should show how people practices improve profitability.
EVP (Employee Value Proposition)	The complete package of rewards, benefits, and opportunities offered to employees.	Serves as the internal "brand promise" for attracting and keeping talent.
HCM (Human Capital Management)	Systems and processes used to manage the entire employee lifecycle.	Provides the technology foundation for HR data and analytics.
HR (Human Resources)	The department that manages employee relations, staffing, and compliance.	The function evolving from administrative to strategic leadership.
HRBP (HR Business Partner)	An HR professional who supports a specific business area as a strategic advisor.	Connects company strategy with team-level execution.
HRIS (Human Resources Information System)	Software used to organize and automate employee and HR data.	Supplies reliable data for reports and analysis.

Term	Definition	Context in Strategic Terms (Simplified)
IP (Intellectual Property)	Intangible assets, such as patents or proprietary ideas, that hold financial value.	Protecting IP depends on retaining key talent and expertise.
M&A (Mergers and Acquisitions)	The process of buying, selling, or combining companies.	HR ensures cultural fit and reduces risk through people due diligence .
P&L (Profit and Loss)	A financial statement showing income and expenses over time.	HR leaders must understand it to connect people results to business results.
PoC (Proof of Concept)	A small project to test whether an idea or tool can solve a business problem.	Used to show measurable success and gain executive buy-in.
PTC (Process-Time-Cost)	A method to measure how time and labor costs are spent on tasks.	Helps calculate inefficiency and justify the need for automation or redesign.
QSR (Quarterly Strategic Review)	A scheduled executive meeting to review progress on strategy and results.	The key accountability session for HR's strategic performance.

Term	Definition	Context in Strategic Terms (Simplified)
ROI (Return on Investment)	The financial return compared to the cost of an investment.	Used to prove the business value of HR programs.
RPE (Revenue Per Employee)	Total company revenue divided by the number of employees.	Measures workforce productivity and efficiency.
SDR (Sales Development Representative)	An entry-level sales role focused on finding new leads or clients.	Often used in HR case studies for turnover or retention strategies.
SLA (Service Level Agreement)	A formal agreement that defines the expected service performance.	HR data can reveal when unmet SLAs cause employee frustration.
TTTP (Time-to-Productivity)	The time it takes a new employee to reach full performance.	Demonstrates the effectiveness of onboarding and training programs.
VP (Vice President)	A senior functional leader overseeing a major business area.	Often a critical partner or influencer in strategic HR initiatives.

Industry Concepts

- **Business Acumen:** The practical knowledge, skill, and judgment required to understand how a business makes money, where costs are incurred, and how operational decisions affect financial results.

- **Causation Analysis:** The process of using data to prove that one factor (e.g., poor management) *directly causes* a negative outcome (e.g., high turnover), rather than just being *correlated* with it.

- **Cost of Regrettable Turnover:** The total measurable expense incurred when a high-performing or critical employee leaves voluntarily. This includes recruitment fees, training costs, and lost productivity revenue.

- **Regrettable Turnover:** The specific loss of high-potential or high-performing employees whose departure directly harms the business.

- **Succession Readiness Score:** A metric showing the percentage of critical leadership or technical roles that have a ready-now internal replacement identified. It measures Talent Risk: the probability of operational failure due to a sudden departure.

- **Talent Forecast:** a predictive plan that models the organization's future talent needs (skills and numbers) based on the business strategy, identifying future Talent Gaps.

- **Talent Risk:** The probability that a lack of necessary skills, leadership, or capacity will severely impact the company's ability to execute its business strategy and maintain operational stability.

- **Turf War (Dynamics):** The friction and conflict that arise when functional leaders perceive a gain in strategic influence as a threat to their autonomy, budget, or data control.

- **Zero-Sum Fallacy:** The mistaken idea that success is a limited resource inside the company. It leads teams to believe that one department's gain (such as receiving a larger budget or faster turnaround) must automatically be another department's loss.

The Horizon: HR's Enduring Strategic Impact

Congratulations. By turning the final page of this book, you have not only absorbed a new framework but have also committed to a new future for yourself and for your organization.

The transition from a tactical operator to a strategic architect is profound. You are no longer just processing transactions; you are shaping the very core of your business's competitive advantage. Your work now directly impacts revenue, innovation, and long-term sustainability.

A Future Built on Strategy

As you move forward, carry this positive truth with you: Strategic HR is the driver of resilient and thriving organizations.

- **Impact:** Your decisions will influence culture, talent quality, and organizational capability for years to come.

- **Value:** You are moving beyond cost-center perception to become a recognized profit and performance multiplier.

- **Opportunity:** The work of a true strategic partnership is never done. It's a continuous journey of measurement, iteration, and growth that promises professional fulfillment and business success.

Embrace the challenge, trust the strategic mindset you have developed, and know that you are now equipped to be a powerful and essential force within your organization.

Connect And Continue The Journey

For ongoing insights, resources, and to join the conversation on the future of strategic HR, please connect with us:

Future Focused HR

info@futurefocusedhr.com

Futurefocusedhr.com

920.415.0508

www.ingramcontent.com/pod-product-compliance
Lightning Source LLC
Chambersburg PA
CBHW061247220326
41599CB00028B/5558